BRITISH MUSEUM

OCCASIONAL PAPER   NUMBER 107

CRAFTS AND TECHNOLOGIES:
SOME TRADITIONAL CRAFTSMEN OF THE
WESTERN GRASSLANDS OF CAMEROON

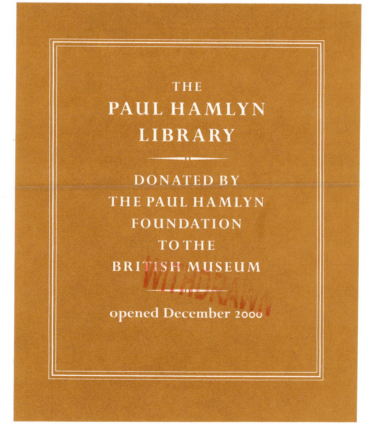
Hans Knöpfli

BRITISH MUSEUM OCCASIONAL PAPERS

Publishers: The British Museum
                      Great Russell Street
                      London WC1B 3DG

Production Editor: Josephine Turquet

Distributors: British Museum Press
                      46 Bloomsbury Street
                      London WC1B 3QQ

Occasional Paper No. 107, 1997

Crafts and Technologies: some Traditional Craftsmen of the Western Grasslands of Cameroon
Hans Knöpfli

ISBN 0 86159 107 0
ISSN 0142 4815

Front cover: A buffalo horn being worked into a title cup, Kedjom Ketingu, 1992,
               (see pages 21, 27)

The Trustees of the British Museum are grateful to the Basel Mission for their contribution towards the production costs of this volume.

In continental Europe copies of this volume can also be obtained from the Basel Mission, CH 4003 Basel, Switzerland; in Cameroon from Presbook, POB 13, Limbe.

For a complete catalogue giving information on the full range of available Occasional Papers please write to:
The Marketing Assistant
British Museum Press
46 Bloomsbury Street
London WC1B 3QQ

Printed and bound in the UK by The Chameleon Press Limited

CONTENTS

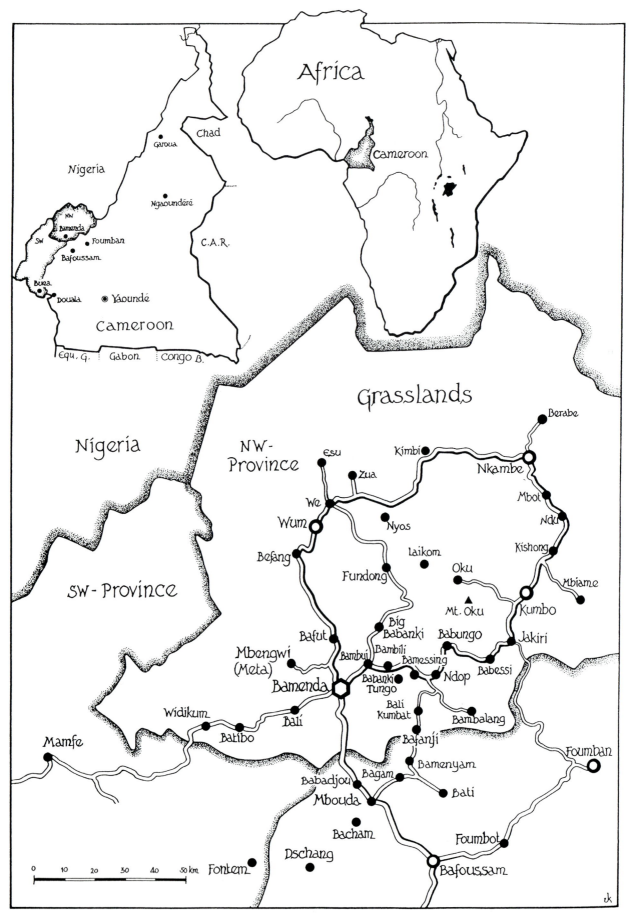

Map of the Western Grasslands of Cameroon

PREFACE

The Western Grasslands, located in the North West Province of the Republic of Cameroon, are bounded in the south by the escarpment that separates them from the tropical rain forest of the South West Province. Their western boundary is part of the Republic of Nigeria. The Adamawa Province marks the northern boundary, and on the east they are bounded by the Western Province. Although the area is inhabited by tribes which speak different languages and dialects, there are common bonds which unite them, for example kingship, which is found in both centralised and decentralised hegemonies alike. Besides, they have common cultural activities as seen in their cultural artefacts.

Since time immemorial, inhabitants of the Western Grasslands have been evolving an educational system devoid of literacy. Contrary to external views about them, the life of these peoples shows that they have been endowed with law, order, and conditions favourable to the production of traditional arts and crafts, including the sciences that made them producers of exquisite works of art which are a result of their refined manners and tastes. For countless generations the youth have been taught different trades thereby producing a class of men and women versed in traditional craftsmanship, who are able to transfer what they learnt to succeeding generations. Besides eking out a livelihood from subsistence agriculture, the various crafts they mastered served them well, as many of them followed trades, vocations and professions that helped in improving the social and economic life of the area.

In preliterate societies, training takes place 'on the job'. The instructors gave their apprentices precise theories which they could retain in their minds as they had no other way of recording them. This has led people in the Western Grasslands, as elsewhere, to develop a strong and retentive memory which has been of great help to them. Besides knowing their trades well, the instructors were, and still are, religiously and culturally well informed, because through the instructions offered, they transmit the beliefs, standards, in fact, the entire cultural ethos of their people to succeeding generations.

The traditional crafts and art works which were taught, included, among other things, weaving, stitching of traditional dress, carving, sculpture, pottery, smelting of metals, and smithing. Traditionally, young people were enthusiastic about apprenticeship in any of these crafts for the sake of interest, and to earn a livelihood. The age-group system practised in the Western Grasslands - whereby children born at roughly the same time grouped themselves under some agreed name for the purpose of helping each other to be good citizens - gave impetus to that enthusiasm. Each age-group disciplined lazy or recalcitrant members, helping them to be duty-conscious and reliable, in order not to destroy the honour of the group. In this way young people prepared themselves to meet the challenges of the life that awaited them in adulthood.

Along with the Christian Faith, brought by the English Baptist Missionary Society to Cameroon in 1845, came Western literary education. Literacy introduced a new type of work into Cameroon society. Before then, Cameroon people had been used to manual vocational work since time immemorial. The young were trained to do manual work. The introduction of literacy brought a new concept of work as it opened the eyes of Cameroonians to see literary vocations through which they could earn a living without involving themselves in the drudgery of manual work. The first people who learnt reading and writing became teachers, preachers, office workers with Government or with business firms, occupations from which they derived income. This made the attraction of literary knowledge captivating to the youth.

In the 1880s, German colonial rule intensified literary education. Literary vocations became much more attractive, setting in motion mobility on a scale hardly experienced in tribal life before. Even illiterates were on the move, looking for manual jobs in plantations, on government stations and in households as cooks and stewards. As the German mark became legal tender in the country, work and commodities were paid for in cash, a thing which revolutionised the economy and social life. Western goods of all sorts, including beverages and schnapps were imported and sold, a thing that increased the desire for 'hot cash'. All these led to the gradual collapse of traditional arts and crafts. Two World Wars, and the teaching of some Christian Missions, which saw traditional cultural artefacts as heathenish and unacceptable to the Christian Faith, accelerated the drop in their production and use.

After World War II, the Rev. Hans Knöpfli, a Swiss missionary, came to Cameroon in the service of the Basel Mission. He was a cabinet maker by training. Working as a Manager of schools, his professional eye helped him quickly to notice a conflict that loomed large between traditional manual and literary vocations. The rudimentary economy was far from any rapid development, not to speak of expansion, due to the ravages of two World Wars. There was not enough work for all the people with school education. Literary education was creating an elitist class in the society which was benefiting from the economy to the disadvantage of the illiterate and semi-literate majority. This was complicated by the dwindling of traditional crafts, creating a vacuum with nothing clear to fill it. The production of cash crops was no solution because it reduced the growth of local food stuffs on which traditional society had depended.

It was in this context, that Rev. Knöpfli's vision of re-awakening traditional crafts as one of the ways out of the economic vacuum began to develop. He believed that traditional crafts would provide work for interested youth. This would help school drop-outs and those who had completed primary school with no hope of finding literary jobs. As it turns out, handicraft production is helping both literates and non-literates alike. There are many secondary, high school, and university graduates who cannot find the jobs appropriate to their education. Added to these are those who complete courses in technical schools, but due to the fact that the economy of the country is in a shambles, find it difficult to secure occupations. Creating interest in manual work will eventually yield economic fruits. Cameroonian literary elites will have to learn to overcome the habit of work discrimination. They hold the wrong view – that being literate excludes them from manual work. As the economy of the country is in difficulties, Cameroonians themselves, especially the literates, have to learn to be producers, as was the case before the arrival of literacy, and stop expecting that Government should do everything for everybody.

It is my ardent hope that the youth of Cameroon will regain interest in manual work, reawaken their enthusiasm for traditional art and crafts, and not depend solely on imported goods, especially cheap plastic material which is difficult to dispose of without causing pollution. They should be patriotic enough to maintain positive aspects of traditional culture. Local production is a sure way of developing and expanding our national economy. This will gradually but surely create chances for self-employment and eventually for the employment for many more young people. What Rev. Hans Knöpfli started over 30 years ago has a future in Cameroon. It now rests with the youth of the country to take advantage of it. This will be an expression of their gratitude to the vision which inspired traditional craftsmen and their techniques.

Rev. Aaron Su, Bafut

INTRODUCTION

This handbook has grown out of my personal involvement in the traditional arts and crafts of the Western Grasslands of Cameroon. Two things have concerned me more than any others. First, the rapid disappearance of the indigenous crafts of the region and second the thousands of bewildered young people who finish school every year. Both have led me to try to preserve the local crafts and the peoples' tradition and skills as a way of relieving under-employment. It was this vision that led to the founding of Prescraft, the organisation of the Presbyterian Church in Cameroon, to promote work in traditional arts and crafts, and sales of quality articles within and outside the Republic of Cameroon.

My intention is to document what I learned during my long involvement with arts and crafts so that:

a) Cameroon's craftsmen and artists are helped to realise that their crafts and techniques are a valuable heritage, to be taken very seriously, and handed down to the next generation.

b) People in Europe and North America become sensitised to the skills, dynamics and symbols of these traditions and cultures, and learn to value them even more highly than many do already.

In view of the book's intended African readership, it is written in English. The core of the book is not tradition in the abstract, but the craftsmen and artists and my continuous respect and love for them.

ACKNOWLEDGMENTS

My first word of gratitude and appreciation goes to the fellowship of the Basel Mission for its interest in the living indigenous cultures of the areas where it operates, its encouragement of my work and its financial support for this publication.

Secondly, I would like to thank my numerous confidants, craftsmen and craftswomen, scattered throughout the Western Grasslands of Cameroon, whose stories and skills this book documents.

Thirdly, my thanks go to the many people who scrutinised my draft manuscripts and worked on improving my English - Mr. Martin and Mrs. Birgit MacMahon, Miss Deirdre MacMahon, Miss Sinead Corr, Mrs. Carol Thalmann, Mrs. Kathryn Landry, Mr. Paul Jenkins and Mr. Jack Chorley. Many people have helped with their expertise in preparing the illustrations for printing, not least Mr. Arthur Scheidegger of Basel. Mr. Ueli Knecht has provided the line drawings.

Fourthly I would like to thank the British Museum for publishing this book in its series of 'Occasional Publications'. I am especially grateful to Dr. Josephine Turquet, the editor of the series, for the interest and energy she has invested in the project, and Dr. Nigel Barley, who took up my MS when it was looking unsuccessfully for a publisher, and has given the text its final polish.

Last, but not least, I thank my wife, Heidi Zingg Knöpfli, who keeps my photographs in order, computerises my texts, and never ceases to encourage me to reflect on my 37 years of experience with the art and artistry of everyday life in the Western Grasslands of Cameroon.

Hans Knöpfli

Editor's Note: Numbers in brackets in the text refer to the illustrations to that particular chapter, all photographs were taken by the author.

Landscape: the road from Ndop to Kumbo

Settlement: Babungo

THE WESTERN GRASSLANDS AND ITS SOCIAL SYSTEM

The Western Grasslands is the name of an area of 16,837 sq km and is formally identical with what is now the North West Province of the Republic of Cameroon. This area covers roughly 40% of Anglophone Cameroon.

This region of the high plateau is of rolling hills and mountains mainly covered with short tough grass and plains covered with high elephant grass. There are steep escarpments, swiftly flowing streams bordered by groves and raphia palms and occasionally forests.

The altitude ranges from 1,200m in Bamenda to over 2,000m in the mountainous areas around Ndu and Nkambe. Rainfall varies from 150-320cm a year and is concentrated in a rainy season from March to October with peak falls in July, August and September. The dry season is characterised by the dry and dusty Harmattan wind blowing from the north-east over the Sahara desert. Travel is easier in the dry season as most of the roads are impassable at times during the heavy rains.

The population is 1,237,348 (census 1987), rather more than half, namely 60%, of the entire population of Anglophone Cameroon. Apart from the natural increase of 2.9% (census 1987) there is also the normal tendency for towns to draw immigrants from the surrounding country. In the Western Grasslands this is particularly noticeable in Bamenda which is the administrative capital. It is situated some 350km from the coast at the centre of a network of smaller roads. Bamenda has a rainfall of 260cm and a temperature range from 12-35 °C.

The basic occupation is subsistence agriculture, carried out mainly by the women, and some cash crops, such as coffee, almost exclusively grown by men. Most of the traditional crafts, for example raphia-weaving, woodcarving and blacksmithing are done by the men; basket-making and pottery by both sexes. Men have adequate time for craft work and at the same time are assured of adequate food supplies through the efforts of their women.

The Western Grasslands area is divided into numerous independent and centralised kingships and chieftainships that vary both in size and population. According to the language atlas (Breton and Fohtung, 1991) 61 languages are spoken in the Western Grasslands alone.

Despite this diversity, all these ethnic groups can be linked in a more or less uniform culture. They constitute bigger or smaller *Fondoms* or chiefdoms. According to history and old tradition there are four *Fondoms*: Bafut, Bali-Nyonga, Kom (since 1992 called Boyo) and Nso, and 57 bigger and smaller chiefdoms.

The presidential decree No. 77/245 of 15 July, 1977, issued by the then State President Amadou Ahidjo ignored the difference between *Fon* and Chief, the two royal titles of traditional rulers. It simply classified all traditional rulers into First, Second and Third Class Chiefs, omitting the title *Fon* altogether. This division was made according to the size of the chiefdoms and the chiefs' educational standards. The chiefs reacted promptly to this decree. Irrespective of their classification, all the chiefs, at least those of the North West Province, called themselves *Fons* and the public followed suit. In everyday language, the title chief has almost disappeared except as 'sub-chief' so that whoever now addresses a traditional ruler as 'Chief' strips him of the honour he is due. Nowadays signboards pointing to palaces, inscriptions on vehicles, letterheads and rubber stamps, etc. have all been changed and labelled with 'His Royal Highness, the *Fon* of ...'.

Within the modern national State of Cameroon the chiefs together with their ethnic groups still constitute traditional, political, social and cultural units.

THE *FON*

The head of the hierarchically structured social system is the traditional ruler, the king, in the Tikar language called *Mfon* or *Fon*. His territory is a *Fondom*. The *Fon* is the highest authority of his ethnic group as well as the master of the earth and the commander of the elements.

As the guardian of tradition he possesses magical power. He is of divine origin hence immortal. It is believed that the *Fon* does not eat solid food and only lives on palm wine.

The Political Position of the *Fon*

As a traditional ruler the *Fon* has to function alongside the Government in Yaoundé in cooperation with the modern state. Despite holding the highest rank at the top of the traditional pyramid and his apparently unlimited power and authority, the *Fon* is not an absolute or despotic ruler. He is the representative of his ethnic group and the symbol of authority, might and power. But he does not hold that power alone. At his side is the Council of Seven (in some ethnic groups it is a Council of Nine): nobles, dignitaries, titleholders in whom the *Fon* has confidence and whose confidence the *Fon*, too, needs. The *Mafo*, the mother of the *Fon* (or one of his sisters, or his first wife), also belongs to the high-ranking titleholders. She is highly respected and has a special role in cases where women are concerned.

The *Fon* can only rule if he has the consent of the Council of Seven and cannot rule without or against them. To do so would be to risk his exalted position and possibly his life, for the seven notables are kingmakers. They enthrone the *Fon*, consequently they can deprive him of his power.

Succession

If the *Fon* grows old and the end of his earthly life is foreseeable, he will choose a successor from amongst his many sons. He does this with the consent of the Council of Seven and the *Mafo*. They keep the choice of the successor secret and will only announce it after 'the fire has gone out in the palace'. The choice made by the *Fon* and the Council is irrevocable so that other princes cannot appeal against this choice. The Council of Seven and the immortalised *Fon* would not tolerate any rivalry, for the *Fon* retains his authority even after having joined his royal ancestors.

Fons are buried in the Sacred House of the palace seated on a stool. If a *Fon* has to take a difficult decision he will bend over the graves of the immortalised *Fons* and ask them for advice, and so *Fons* who 'have gone' are always present

and the *Fon* is in magical conjunction with his royal ancestors and acts as mediator between them and his people. It is one of the *Fon*'s duties to offer sacrifices to these royal ancestors.

THE SECRET SOCIETIES
(also called Regulatory Societies)

Apart from the Council of Seven, the *Fon* also has secret societies at his side. Only adult, well-to-do men of unstained reputation and of high social standing are eligible for membership of such societies. Influential positions are hereditary e.g. those of sub-chief, head of village ward and head of family. A title conferred for personal merit is a rare, but possible, exception.

Sacred cult objects are kept in the custody of these societies and are used to carry out their political, legal, economic and social functions. A society or association is called secret because it conceals its rites and activities from those who are not members. Of all the secret societies *KwiFon*, popularly called *Ngumba*, is the most dreaded. It is the supreme traditional authority charged with passing and executing judgment in serious cases and even the *Fon* is subject to its authority so that *KwiFon* constitutes another political counterweight to the *Fon*.

THE TRADITIONAL ELITE

All the title holders, nobles and dignitaries constitute the traditional elite. They possess remarkable power for they are the holders of many rights and privileges. Their elite positions are often emphasised by numerous art objects so that social statuses are probably most clearly seen in material culture.

THE ART OF THE COURT

The art of the Western Grasslands is a court art based on complicated protocol and numerous rituals. Art is created in the service of the *Fon* and his elite and strengthens the respect and admiration considered appropriate to them and their supporters. Thus art contributes indirectly to the welfare of the entire people. Art and cult objects are insignia but there are also prestige pieces made just for show that emphasise the importance and wealth of the *Fon* and his retinue.

Symbols of power are limited to office holders so that they constitute an 'art of leadership'. The traditional world view and fundamental beliefs of the Grasslands are manifest in the court art which links different generations in an ongoing pattern. Thus it represents a kind of collective memory.

THE SKIN-COVERED DRUM

Kiefeh Wembai (born *c.* 1932) of Babungo Ibia quarter, Ndop Sub-Division (since 1992 Ngokentugia Division) is a woodcarver and expert in the production of skin-covered drums. These are upright drums of different sizes (from approximately 20cm in height and 15cm in diameter to about 130cm in height and 70cm in diameter). They consist of a rough length of tree-trunk which is hollowed out, the side shaped in a great variety of forms and usually decorated with traditional symbols carved in low relief. The upper, wider end is then covered with an animal skin, preferably that of an antelope.

Kiefeh Wembai has a widespread reputation as the best drummaker of the area. In more than 30 years during which I have been engaged with handicrafts of the Western Grasslands, there is no other article which has given me and the whole Prescraft project such enormous problems as the upright skin-covered drum. Though every village and village ward has them in large numbers (they are kept by the very same men who keep the masks), there is hardly anything so rare as a good-sounding skin-covered drum. In every tribal area there is a handful of drummakers, but hardly any of them can make a long-lasting drum that retains its sound quality. I have visited many of the drummakers in the North West Province and studied their techniques and tried to divine the secret of that indefinable something which makes a good drum. It would take too long to show in detail the many slight differences between different experts and the way they apply their knowledge to the practical task of drummaking.

After I had made the acquaintance of Kiefeh Wembai, I decided to forsake all other drummakers and concentrate on this man who showed the most impressive skills. Since that time I have bought many drums from him, and hardly any of them 'went down', i.e. their skins remained taut, and if after some time one did lose its tension, he put it right with the skill of a true master of his craft.

Without getting lost in incidentals, the basic determinants of a good drum are:
- the choice of the correct type of wood;
- the seasoning, i.e. drying of the wood;
- the choice of the right type of skin;
- the preparation of the skin;
- the technique of spanning the skin on the drum.

The drums made by Kiefeh Wembai are not only superb as far as the tautness of the skin and consequently its sound are concerned but to an expert's eye, they are also of attractive appearance, i.e. they show good and careful work on the body (1).

Though I had been a good and regular customer of his over the years and had often watched him working, he showed some reluctance when I asked his permission to interview him on his life and work and to take pictures of the process of drummaking. But when I assured him that I did not intend to steal his trade but rather to record his technique for posterity because it is the best I have seen anywhere, the usual friendly smile returned to his face. We arranged to meet on Tuesday, 14 May 1991, in his compound before 8 a.m.

SOME GENERAL POINTS ON DRUMMAKING

The Type of Wood Used

Kiefeh Wembai emphasised that only one of the locally available species of tree can be chosen for drums, and that is *ibo'* in the Babungo, or *mbangom* in the Mungaka language (*Cordia platythyrsa*). It is the wood used far and wide for stools, statues and masks because it does not readily crack, is semi-hard and whitish-yellow in colour.

The Seasoning of the Wood

Like any other wood carver, Kiefeh Wembai does not work with wood which has been left to season for years, as was the original practice. Nowadays, the trees are felled, chopped, or in some cases sawn, into logs, left in the forest for a couple of weeks 'until the water is out', transported home by head load and immediately worked into drums and stools. Large objects which require a big, heavy log are roughly worked in the bush for easier transportation home. But unlike other carvers and producers, Keifeh Wembai has invented a simple but special way, which I have seen nowhere else, of drying the hollowed and shaped drum-bodies over the fire. He hangs the drum-bodies (before spanning the skin) upside down over the large fire-place where a fire is kept burning day and night. The drying time depends on the size of the drums. A small drum of about 40-60cm in height may remain there for three to four days while a large, heavy drum is left there for up to two weeks to complete drying. Only after this initial process can the skin be applied, because it is now certain that the wood will no longer shrink. The shrinkage of unseasoned wood is one of the main causes of drums with slack skins.

The Type of Skin to be Used for Drums

Kiefeh Wembai assured me that he would only use the skins of antelope, *fratambos* and deer, though they are not easily obtained nowadays. He has people who bring the skins to him from all over Cameroon and even from neighbouring countries. That is why he always needs advance payment when he makes drums for such scarce skins are expensive.

The Preparation of the Skin

Depending on the thickness of the skin, it has to be soaked in water for 24 to 48 hours. A skin may be kept in the water for too short or for too long a time. If for too short a time the 'threads' in the skin (the capillaries - blood vessels - that form an interconnecting network all over the inner side of the skin) are not yet soft enough and it cannot be stretched over the drum sufficiently; consequently the sound is not good. On the other hand if the skin is kept in water too long, the veins rot and the skin will be overstretched when force is applied to span the skin over the drum.

The technique for applying the skin to the drum is the most important part of the work and will be explained and illustrated in detail below.

THE SEQUENCE OF OPERATIONS IN MAKING A DRUM

- The tree is felled and the trunk cut into logs in rough lengths, and then transported home by head load after the logs have 'lost their water'. Keifeh Wembai still does it with an axe while some others use a chain saw.
- The log is stripped of its bark (2), either end trimmed at right angles (3), and then set upright in a hole in the ground (4) and hollowed, initially by means of a native axe (5) followed by chisels of different lengths: two to four days' work.
- The log receives its rough shape which shows a division into an upper and a lower part (6) followed by the finishing of the outer shape: one to two days' work.
- The hollowed and shaped drumbody is hung over the fire to dry for 3-14 days (7).
- The antelope skin is chosen (8) and then soaked in water for 24-48 hours.
- Depending on the circumference of the drum 6-14 holes are burnt into the upper part (9). They are approximately 3-4 fingers-width below the rim of the drummouth. A hot round iron is used which is as thick as the third or fourth finger of the human hand. The tapered pegs required are prepared. Kiefeh Wembai gets the raphia fibres and bush rope ready and blackens part of the drumbody by means of hot flat irons (10). The irons are heated in a charcoal fire with the help of a pair of hand-bellows (11). This is the work of one to two days.

Before we describe the process of applying the skin to the drum, let us look at the equipment he is using for this work:
- four to six heavy stones of approx. 30-40kg each, framed with wire and iron bands;
- four to six iron hooks (on which to hang the stones);
- a hoop made of a bushrope needed for the fastening of the skin;
- raphia fibres to join the hoop;
- needle and thread (the latter originally made of bushropes, nowadays often nylon thread);
- palm oil;

- a skin from either an antelope, a deer or a *fratambo*;
- nails made of Indian bamboo (nowadays often wire nails);
- three long sticks to support the drums sideways;
- a mallet;
- a strong round iron bar about 60cm in length with one end pointed;
- plaited fibre ropes.

PROCESS OF SPANNING THE SKIN ON THE DRUM

- The equipment is set out within easy reach.
- A hoop is made from the bushrope: the circumference of the drumbody is measured with the rope and it is trimmed to the correct length cutting the ends with a slanted cut so that they fit together exactly. The joint is tied with raphia fibres (12).
- The mouth of the drum is smeared with palm oil (13) to make the skin glide over it smoothly (14).
- The skin is taken out of the water and put over the mouth of the drum.
- The ready-made hoop is placed over the skin and pressed down with both hands as far as it can go. The skin is drawn down as much as possible by hand (14).
- The edges of the skin are bent upwards. This means that the pegs and the hoop which maintain the tension of the skin are always attached to the doubled skin. For the moment, three nails are driven through the skin into the drumbody just above the hoop thus preventing the hoop from running back.
- The hoop is stitched to the hide with a needle and thread (15); on this occasion nylon thread was used because there was no time to go to the bush to find the plant from whose bark thread is made. Gaps of 8-12cm are left between the stitches (16).
- The circumference of the drumbody is measured with a strip of plantain bark and the circumference is divided into six equal parts (first the rope is folded into two halves and then each half into three equal parts).
- This plantain skin-rope is placed round the

drumbody and the six points are marked. At each point, an iron hook is inserted into the skin just above the ring.
- The upright drumbody is balanced on three long sticks.
- One of the heavy stones is hung on one of the six hooks, then the second, third, fourth, fifth and sixth always making sure that the whole thing does not get out of balance (17).
- The hoop is knocked down using a mallet and a special piece of wood which looks like a blunt wedge, going along the hoop around the drum (18).
- A plaited fibre rope is placed round the drum just above the ring.
- The pointed end of the iron bar is pushed through the plaited rope and the skin underneath and while slanted from above is forced into one of the six holes already made in the drumbody. Using the bar as a lever, the hoop to which the skin has been fastened is pressed down. The iron bar is held in position with the left hand, while the first of the tapered pegs is inserted into the same hole with the right hand (19). As the iron bar is gradually withdrawn, the peg is pushed into the hole. Once the peg is in its right position it is knocked into place - and so on with the other pegs, one after the other. A drum of approximately 25cm diameter takes 6 pegs, one of 30cm diameter 9 pegs and up to 14 pegs for larger drums.
- The heavy stones are removed one after the other, always making sure that the drum does not fall over by changing the positions of the supporting sticks as necessary.
- The iron-hooks are removed and surplus skin is cut off (20).
- The hair of the skin is shaved off with a razor blade (21). (Formerly locally made shaving knives were used for shaving beards and animal skins.)
- A second plaited rope is stitched round the drum on top of the first one (22).
- Finally the whole drumbody is rubbed with palm oil mixed with camwood powder (23).

The tools used to prepare the drumbody are axe, adze, cutlass, chisels of different lengths, and mallet (all made locally apart from the axe and the cutlass).

One question remains to be answered: How is the spanning of the skin done on small drums? Small drums of up to about 80cm in height are raised on a wooden pedestal so that the big stones can be hung on the skin as described above. In the centre of the wooden base a protruding thick stick is fitted over which the drum is set. This stick helps to centre the drum and to keep the drum from falling over (24).

All pictures in this chapter concern the expert drummaker Kiefeh Wembai. They were taken in his compound at Babungo-Ibia quarter in May 1991, except for Nos 8-11 which date from December 1991.

1 The bodies of the completed drums are given a good finish.

2 The log is denuded of its bark.

3 The log is trimmed at right angles.

4 The log is stood in a hole in the ground.

9

5 The log is hollowed out.

6 The log is shaped.

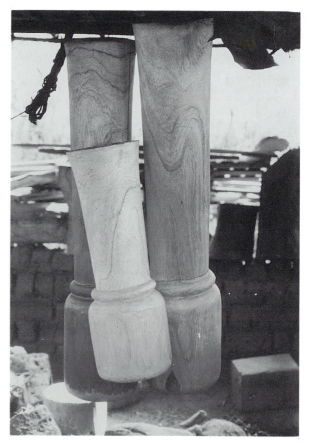

7 The hollowed logs are dried.

8 The most suitable antelope skin is chosen.

9 The peg-holes are burnt into the drumbody.

10 The drumbody is beautified by partial blackening.

11 The irons are heated in the charcoal fire with the help of a pair of hand-bellows.

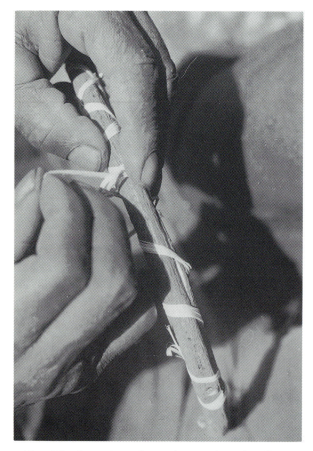

12   The hoop is tied together with raphia fibres.

13   The mouth is smeared with palm oil.

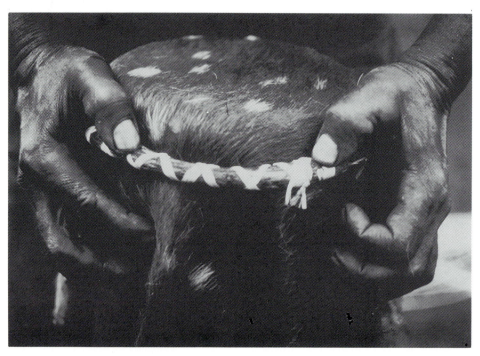

14   The hoop is put over the wet skin and pressed down to stretch it.

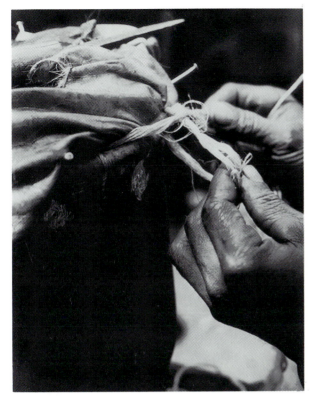

15   The hoop is stitched to the skin.

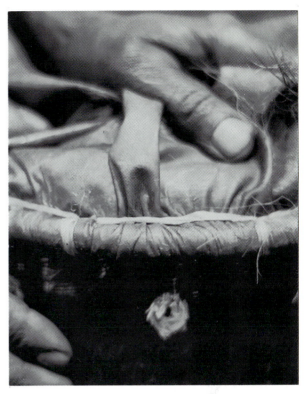

16   Large gaps are left between the stitches.

17   Heavy stones are hung on iron hooks to stretch the skin.

18   The hoop is hammered down.

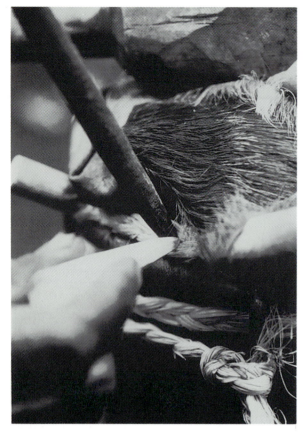

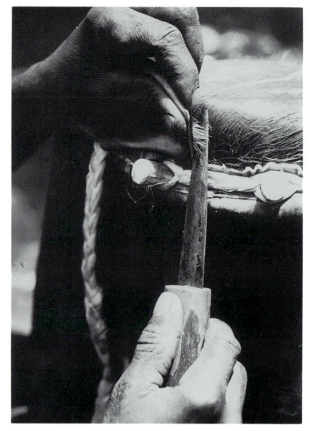

19   The hoop is pressed down in order to insert the pegs.

20   The surplus skin is cut off.

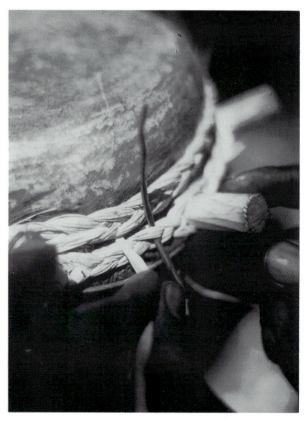

21   The hair is shaved from the skin.

22   A second plaited rope is stitched onto the first one.

23 Camwood powder is mixed with palm oil.

24 Small drums are raised for the stretching of the skin.

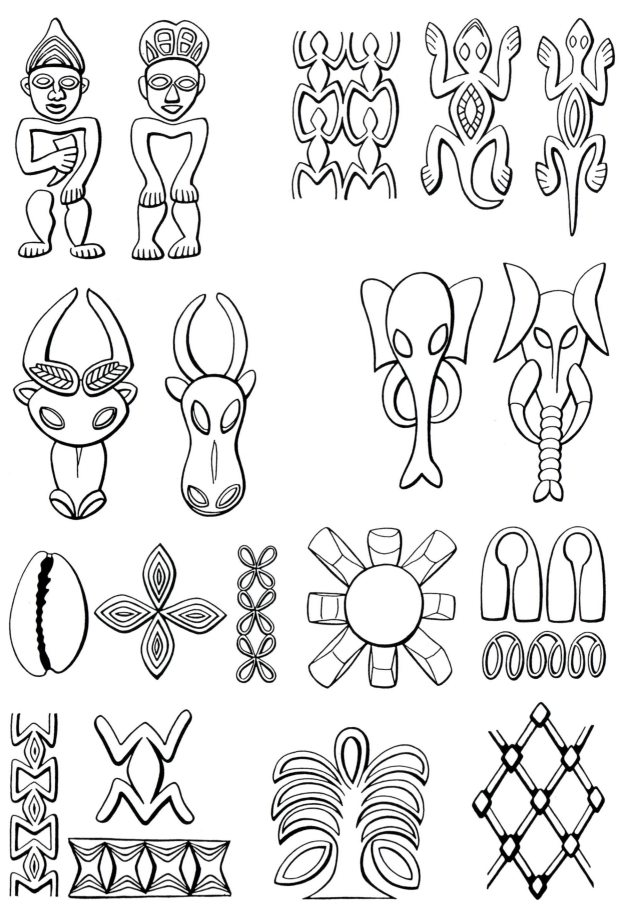

Motifs carved on title cups

THE TITLE CUP

The title cup is a drinking horn. Title cups come in various grades:

Grade one: the carved buffalo horn used by dignitaries such as *Fons*, sub-chiefs and kingmakers;

Grade two: the dwarf cow horn used by the head of the family;

Grade three: the deer horn used by kingmakers who have no buffalo horn;

Grade four: the cow horn used by commoners, both men and women.

By tradition, the title cup is the most precious heirloom handed down to the most honourable member of the family from one generation to the next. Every extended family possesses such a title cup.

INITIATION OF A NEW TITLE CUP

A new title cup must never be brought into use without due ceremony. Elderly men who know the ritual appropriate to each rank are invited to perform it. The first question they ask is, 'Are all the required things ready?' Depending on rank, the requirements include food, palm wine, and cocks or goats. The soup must be prepared by men only, or by elderly women who are ritually clean. If all is in order, the highest-ranking man pours palm wine into the new cup. He uses it to offer a libation on the graves of the deceased fore-fathers, invoking these ancestors to be witnesses to the ceremony, promising them that the new title cup will care for the entire family and maintain it. He then drinks from the cup and passes it round the men present, making sure that it is not emptied. The cup is then handed over to the rightful owner, who drains it. The honour of emptying the cup is the owner's and his alone since the man who does so is held to know all the secrets of the family, even the most intimate. In private, the title holder may honour his friends by letting them drink from his cup, but this is never done in public or on ceremonial occasions.

As a rule women are not allowed to drink from the cup but the owner may pour palm wine from it into a woman's palms from which she then drinks the wine. Again this is forbidden when a woman is unclean. A woman is regarded as unclean for seven days when she has her monthly period. Men are considered unclean for three days after sexual intercourse as they might unknowingly have had contact with an unclean woman.

THE SIGNIFICANCE OF THE TITLE CUP

Of all of the traditional regalia of a title holder, including the stool and cap, the title cup is the most important. The reasons for its special significance are numerous.

- From the moment a successor has the cup in his hands he has all the rights of his late forefathers. However, he must take great care that he does not violate the rules of the cup. On the one hand it may be used for cleansing and healing purposes. On the other hand it may be used for cursing a family member who has gone astray. That is why the title cup is highly respected as an instrument of blessing but also feared as an instrument of danger. Some examples may illustrate this:

A sickly child may be made to drink from the title cup in the hope that the ancestors may take special care of the child and make it whole.

In a traditional marriage ceremony, the title holder gives the cup first to his daughter to drink from. She gives it to her husband but on no account must they empty it. The title holder then pours a libation invoking the ancestors to bless the couple and the covenant they have made with one another and with the ancestors. At the same time, the wife is threatened with a curse should she leave her husband without due cause.

The cup is regarded as having been violated if a woman drinks from it without permission, or the owner uses it foolishly in a bar for beer. In the latter case, the owner himself will be struck by a curse. It is believed that a traditional sickness, such as epilepsy, impotence or barrenness of his wife (or wives) will befall him.

- If the mouth of the cup is no longer smooth, it is believed to be a sign that the mouth has been eaten by the lips of the ancestors.

- The cup is the sign of the covenant between the ancestors and the family. It is believed that when the title holder drinks from the cup he drinks wine from his forefathers and that their breath is around it.

- It is believed that when family members who have gone astray desire to drink from the cup their wrongdoings are washed away by their forefathers who see all things much more clearly and completely than the living. If the title cup is used for forgiving, cleansing and healing purposes the person concerned, after due libation and invocation, drinks from the cup and empties it.

- In judgments, the cup stands for the presence and authority of the forefathers, especially of the founding ancestor of the family. He is the most important for he is next to god. (The traditional god is the supreme being who is approached through intermediaries, such as the ancestors.)

- The cup is the sign of reconciliation between two parties. After judgment has been passed in a dispute the title holder asks those concerned, 'Are you satisfied with the judgment?' If not, the palaver continues until a consensus is reached. If the answer is 'yes' then the title holder pours a libation over the graves of the ancestors. Then he drinks from the cup and pours wine into the palms of those concerned which they drink in the belief that if someone goes against the judgment a curse will be placed on them.

- If a dispute in the family has been settled by the title holder, the only way to know that all the members are really at peace again is by their communally drinking from the title cup. (It is understood that only palm wine is used for such purposes.)

- The title cup may be used to put a curse on someone. For instance the following two occurrences were reported from Bafut.

- A title holder asked a man, 'Is it true that you made this woman pregnant?' Answer, 'No'. 'Then drink from this cup.' The man drank and shortly afterwards he became blind. No treatment either from native doctors or from eye-specialists could cure the man's blindness. He is still alive – blind.

- A youngster left for Douala on his own, leaving behind his old, helpless mother. After a certain length of time the young man was called back by the title holder for judgment. Finally the head of the family filled his cup with palm wine and splashed the wine into the young mans's face saying, 'Cursed be you'.

- The title cup is so important because it is used to offer a sacrifice to the heads of the ancestors. In case of sickness in the family, misfortune in business, failure in school, accident, etc., the family members first of all consult the diviner. He may say, 'Your late father is annoyed because he is hungry for *mimbo* (palm wine) which you failed to give him'. So the family is called together and they bring a cock, palm oil, camwood and palm wine. The title holder will slaughter the cock and drop the blood over the stones (which mark the departeds' heads). Then he pours some palm oil on the stones, rubs them with camwood and eventually pours wine from the title cup over them.

- Despite the title cup's importance, it is not the first part of the traditional insignia to be handed over to a successor. This occurs in the following order: first, the stool to sit on; second, the cap as a sign of respect; and only third the title cup to unite the family. These three objects are important for every title holder, for in every family meeting they must be present so as to speak as witnesses to the departed. If one of these objects is not seen, especially the title cup, there will be a problem. Members will refuse to drink from another cup. Consequently the family splits. What tends to happen nowadays is that in order to get money the head of the family may secretly dispose of his heirlooms, the worst offence being to dispose of his cup, for the cup belongs to all the family members, whilst the stool and cap are for the title holder alone. If the title cup is really missing, it is believed that the title holder risks losing his life and family members may begin to die, one after the other. Therefore the cup has to be handled very carefully.

- If the title holder leaves his village, the eldest family member (it may be a woman for elderly women are always ritually clean) pours wine from the title cup over the feet of the departing head of the family, passing on to him the blessings of the family thus, 'May our ancestors be with you. Go with their blessing and bring peace into every house wherever you go'.

THE TECHNIQUE OF CARVING A BUFFALO HORN

After several failed attempts to study buffalo horncarving with the artist Philip Nkọsụ Vubom at Kedjom Keku in the 1960s and 1970s, I tried again in January 1991. Philip was at that time the sole horncarver known to me. I had made his acquaintance first of all through the late *Fon* Vubangsi and also through Philip's father Rev. John Nkọsụ (now deceased) with whom I had shared church work in the Bafut-Ndop area for several years. Rev. John Nkọsụ was a pastor and at the same time a renowned wood-carver. For these reasons I was in close contact with the Nkọsụ family at Kedjom Keku. In the 1960s horncarving was still a lucrative business and at that time a good number of buffalos remained in the forests behind the village of Esu in the Menchum Division (1).

Philip used to go there to buy the raw horns which he then carved at home. Whenever he had completed half a dozen, he came to Bali-Nyonga to sell them. We used to buy the carved horns from him and sold them to indigenous people as well as expatriates and tourists.

Many a time I tried to persuade him to show me both the preparation of a horn and the actual work of carving. While he always reacted with vague agreement, whenever I tried to make a firm arrangement he made an excuse. This made me realise that he did not want me to see him work on horns.

Over a decade later, I arranged with *Fon* Vugah II to come to his village to do some field work. The *Fon* himself summoned the craftsmen I wished to see, among them my old friend Philip. This time he readily agreed to let me see him work on horns. I tried to pin him down by giving him two raw horns which, I knew, must be kept in water for not less than three weeks before carving can start and we agreed on the most suitable day for me to come.

On that day, Philip welcomed me by saying that he had reconsidered his decision to let me see his work, for according to an old traditional law which goes back to one of the late *Fons*, the art of horncarving must remain a secret revealed only to those who had been duly initiated into it. Even the *Fon* himself did not succeed in changing Philip's mind. I finished my other work in Kedjom Keku and went back to Bamessing determined not to abandon my wish to see the process of horncarving.

I started afresh enquiring whether there might be someone among the numerous wood-carvers in the nearby village Kedjom Ketingu who knew how to carve a horn. Two names were given to me and I did not hesitate to contact them: one was John Viuyen Vemessi, aged about 60, wood- and horncarver and farmer.

I learnt carving from my father: stools, statues, pillars, drums, elephant tusks and buffalo horns. Horncarving was interesting when buffalo horns were still available. I used to carve them continuously as my daily job and lived by it. But now I no longer have an interest in it since the horns are not readily available. I did not even know where the horns came from for the customers supplied them to me. Even wood-carving, which was an interesting job, has diminished because of the scarcity of trees. Nowadays, a tree which can give ten stools costs CFA 5000 in Kedjom Ketingu. Formerly we did not pay money for trees. Instead we paid in kind. For a tree which supplied wood for about ten stools I used to carve one in return. With all these problems I have lost interest in both wood-carving and horncarving and concentrate more on farming. Nowadays, I just do carving for special customers and as a sort of pleasure in my leisure time. In this way I agree to carve the horn which you have brought to me. I shall work on it in the evenings, therefore be patient.

We then fixed a day for me to come and see him start work.

With the second horn, I went to the second man, Ndoh Neya, aged about 68, who lives in an another quarter (Buh-Kejong) in Kedjom Ketingu. After the usual lengthy greeting ceremony I mentioned the purpose of my coming and when I removed the buffalo horn from my bag his face lit up.

> For quite some time I have not seen a horn. You know that nowadays buffalos are not seen here in Kedjom Ketingu and so the horns are not easily available. The horn alone is costly and the carving difficult. That is why only rich big men can afford to buy and use a carved buffalo horn as their drinking cup. Moreover there are very strict laws in our tradition with regard to the use of such a cup. Only the *Fon*, sub-chiefs, kingmakers and 'chop-chairs' are permitted to use it. This is so even up to today.

Since the day I had fixed with John Vemessi was their 'country Sunday', I proposed to Ndoh Neya that I would come on the following day to see for myself his special work with the horn.

On the agreed day I was at John Vemessi's door at 6 p.m. He was at home, a promising sign, but then he told me that he had changed his mind. Under no circumstances could he allow me to see this work. 'It is our belief that when preparing a horn for carving other persons must not see it for fear that they may have some bad *juju* or witchcraft on them which can make the horn crack while heating it over the fire.' I went home that evening rather sad.

The following morning I proceeded to Ndoh Neya to try my luck with him. He, too, brought forth several excuses for not starting today. However, he promised to start work on the following day at 6 a.m. I asked myself: Why so early? Does he think that I will not get up at 5 a.m?

The following morning I entered his compound full of hope and anxiety at 6 a.m. prompt. The first thing he did was to pin his spear, with a piece of knotted grass tied to it, into the hard ground about 4m away from his house-door. He explained to me later that this was to scare away unwanted visitors and witches who could come to either steal his trade or to spoil his work. Since he had to use fire he did not work in his house but in the house of his wife and children, for only in his

wife's house is there a fireplace. On this morning, therefore, his wife had to improvise a fireplace in the open air to cook our meal. After he had been working successfully for two consecutive hours, he showed great relief, turned to me and said, 'Thank you. You are a man with one heart (a good man), for, if you had two hearts, the horn would have cracked or I would have mistakenly burnt a hole into it. Since the cup has come out of the fire whole, I agree to co-operate with you'.

Ndoh Neya agreed that I should always come on a country Sunday, i.e. every eighth day and so I did over seven weeks until he had completed work on the horn. Here then is a brief description of how Ndoh Neya worked a raw buffalo horn into a carved drinking horn within the space of seven weeks.

WORKING THE HORN

14th February 1992: as agreed we met at 6.30 a.m. in his compound, which consists of two houses, his and his wife's. He wanted to start this early because of the coolness of the morning hours since he had to work with fire.

In one of the dark corners of his own house, was an old earthen pot filled with water in which he had been keeping the horn for several weeks in order to soften it (2). Apparently he kept other things in the water for it took him quite some time to find my horn among the other things. The water was black and stinking. He gathered his tools and a basket with other equipment (3) and I followed him over to his wife's house. There we sat opposite each other, the fireplace between us. There were still some embers under the wood ash. With dry maize leaves and some light pieces of raphia bark and pith he poked the embers and blew into them until they caught fire.

He then forced a tapered round stick of about 30cm length into the base of the softened horn and added more sticks until he had achieved the opening he wanted (4). With a soaked rag clipped in a pair of raphia tongs, he applied castor oil thickly over the entire surface of the horn (5) and then warmed it over the fire for about five minutes. The castor oil on the horn's surface dried out in the heat, leaving behind a parched crust.

Castor oil was applied for a second time and the warming over the fire repeated until all the castor oil was parched and charred (6). Now he forced additional wedges, which he had prepared previously out of raphia bark, between the round tapered stick and the mouth of the horn in order to widen it. Castor oil was applied for the third time starting from the pointed end and only covering about half of the horn. This same half was warmed again over the fire, then he took it over to a corner of the room and laid an old carved stool on the floor so that the purposely made hole was on the upper side. He put the thin end of the horn into the hole of the stool. Holding the lever in his hands and using rags to protect them, he bent and straightened the horn forwards, backwards and sideways until it had acquired its desired shape (7). During this process, he poured cold water over the horn every now and then, especially over the part that he wanted to bend. Having shaped the horn successfully and satisfactorily he put it back into the water pot from which he had removed it.

About 30 minutes later he took it out again and knocked the stick and the wedges out as the horn was now cold and holding its new shape firmly. Looking at the horn proudly and turning it in his hands to examine it, he walked over to his house and put the horn back into the softening water.

While Ndoh Neya was working I asked him the following questions and recorded his answers.

- What is the purpose of soaking a raw horn in cold water for three weeks?
  Answer: To make it soft.
- What is the purpose of applying castor oil to the horn before warming it over the fire?
  Answer: First, so that the horn does not get burnt, and second, to make the horn soft as the heat of the fire makes part of the oil penetrate the horn.
- Why are only buffalo horns carved in this way?
  Answer: The buffalo horn is thicker than any other animal horn. That is why it was chosen for carving and thus became the title cup of the first grade dignitaries. We have tried to carve other horns but failed.

Eight days later, again on the country Sunday, I went to Ndoh Neya once more. This time his working tool was a big cutlass. With it he trimmed off the upper part of the horn which by nature is thin and irregular. He cut the fairly soft material down to the desired size and shape. Keeping the horn upside down, he cleaned off the crust of charred castor oil and the outer layer of the horn (8). He then carved six notches into the thick upper concave part of the horn directly under the spot where the spout still had to be shaped. Castor oil was applied once more on thick, rough places of the horn, and having warmed it over the fire (9), he cleaned the surface with the cutlass for the last time. This was all that was done on this day. He put the horn back into the water pot.

Before I met him again eight days later he had smoothed the entire surface of the horn with his penknife, but purposely delayed the shaping of the spout until I was present.

Having again softened the horn in water for another eight days, Ndoh Neya demonstrated to me the shaping of the spout as follows: he fetched the same old stool which he had used for bending the horn. Sitting on a stone he placed the stool upright in front of him facing the smaller of the two cracks in the seat. He then pressed the rim of the horn into the wide opening of the natural crack (10). He took his time, waiting till the horn was hard enough again to hold the shape of what I term the 'spout', although it is not used as such.

When drinking from the cup or pouring out wine for a libation this is done either from the opposite side of the horn or from one side (11). The so called 'spout' is simply an additional embellishment, just as the notches are on the upper concave part.

That day the horn was too hard to be engraved and had to be soaked for at least another night before Ndoh Neya could start work (12, 13) with his locally made tools (14). In this way he continued to completion: after every three hours' work the horn had to be put back into water (15).

RELIEF SYMBOLS ON TITLE CUPS

Traditionally, a man's drinking cup is the mark of his social position in the society so that it is a status symbol *par excellence*. The horn of commoners is the cut-off end of the long horn of the zebu, whereas the nobles and title holders have cups made out of buffalo horn which is a royal animal in the tradition of the Western Grasslands. The undecorated buffalo horn is not a title cup, however. Black and hard as tropical ebony wood, sometimes with a dark olive tinge, it is always worked upon and richly embellished with symbols of the rank of the owner.

The most frequent symbols and associated meanings are:

- the elephant head: royal might and dignity (20);
- the buffalo head: royal power; danger (20, 21);
- the male figure/head with a prestige cap: nobility (18, 22);
- the earth spider (usually eight legs): accumulated knowledge, wisdom (19, 21);
- the hunting net (an x-like cross): unity (23);
- the lizard: liveliness, abundant life (16, 20, 22, 25);
- the frog: fertility, prosperity, life (17);
- the cowrie: royal dignity, membership of ngumba (16, 19, 24);
- the double gong: supreme authority (16, 24);
- the palm tree: prosperity, wealth (21).

Notes on the Illustrations

Illustrations 16,17,18 Such symbols usually appear in meaningful combinations. Thus, the illustrations 16, 17 and 18 are photographs of one and the same title cup belonging to Gwejui Bah (born *c.* 1926) of Babungo-Mbuakang, Ndop. Gwejui Bah comes second to the *Fon* of Babungo. He was the one who put the present *Fon* Zofoa II on the throne in 1954.

The combination of two double-gongs, two times four cowries and a lizard and all these on either side of the title cup indicate Gwejui Bah's royal authority, royal dignity and wealth and abundant life: many wives, a host of children among which are several pairs of twins.

The chain of stylised frogs on the back of the horn stands for being blessed with a big extended family for which he needs an ever increasing yield of farm produce to keep his several generations of blood relatives alive.

The full upright male figure under the spout wearing a prestige cap is an absolute indication that the owner has practically unlimited authority in the society.

It is furthermore of importance to know that any title cup with either a male figure or a male head on it indicates that no other person than the owner is allowed to drink from that cup.

Peter Vamessi of Kedjom Ketingu carved this horn soon after the World War I. Blind though he is, our discussion was fairly fluent. He is said to be about 100 years old.

Illustration 19 The entire cup carries only two designs: the earth spider and the cross-shaped cowrie shells. The combination of wisdom and royal dignity marks out a member of ngumba.

Illustration 20 On both sides of the horn the patterns of lizard, elephant and buffalo symbolise respectively the owner's abundant life, might, power and danger.

Illustration 21 On this title cup the three symbols buffalo, earth spider and palm tree representing the power, wisdom and prosperity of the titleholder.

Illustration 22 The male head with distinctive cap, the lizard and the earth spider signify a wise and lively member of the royal house.

Illustration 23 This title cup with the symbol of the hunting net in the hands of the head of a family points to the twofold challenge of caring for both well-being and unity within the clan.

Illustration 24 Both sides of the title cup bear the emblems of the cross-shaped cowrie shells and the double-gong i.e. these are symbols of supreme authority in the hands of a member of ngumba.

Illustration 25 This title cup, depicting nothing but lizards, is unique. It belongs to the head of a large, extended family, i.e. abundant life indeed.

Illustration 26 A collection of five title cups which I requested from Bali-Nyonga nobles to allow me to photograph after a grand death festival.

Two observations are necessary here. The first concerns the most frequent symbol seen on title cups, the cowrie shell. Because of its importance as symbol of royal dignity and wealth, it is seen on practically every title cup (see illustrations 13, 15, 16, 19, 24). Some interpreters, however, seem to have been misled by the usual arrangement of the cowries in fours to see in it either a four-leaf flower or even a crossroads. Informants have told me that both interpretations are far-fetched and non-traditional.

In fact, the cross-shaped arrangement in the pattern of four cowrie shells has its counterpart on the black cap worn by members of ngumba (27),

signifying much greater authority than comes from material wealth.

The second observation concerns the style of horncarving. As far as I am aware, there is only one prevailing style in the Western Grasslands: that of Kedjom Keku/Kedjom Ketingu. Of course, within the one style, slightly different hands can be distinguished. A different style, however, originates from Bamoum. The photograph of a horn carved in Foumban (28) shows clearly the difference between the two styles.

11   The correct way of drinking from a title cup, Babungo-Mbuakang, January 1992

Illustrations to the Title Cup: with the exception of illustration 11 the photographs 1–15 concern horncarver Ndoh Neya and were taken in his compound at Kedjom Ketingu between January and March 1992.

1 Buffalo heads being dried

2 The raw horn is soaked in water.

3 Tools and equipment

4 The mouth of the horn is widened.

5 Castor oil is applied.

6 The horn is heated over the fire.

7 The horn is shaped.

8 The crust is cleaned off.

9 The horn is reheated (showing the six notches).

10   The spout is shaped.

12   Carving the horn

Note: *for illustration 11 see page 23.*

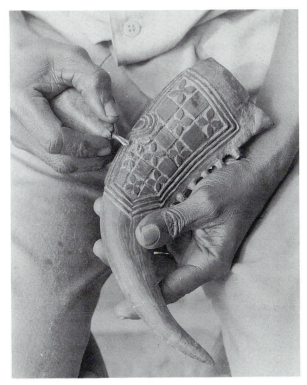

13   Carving the horn

14   Locally made carving tools

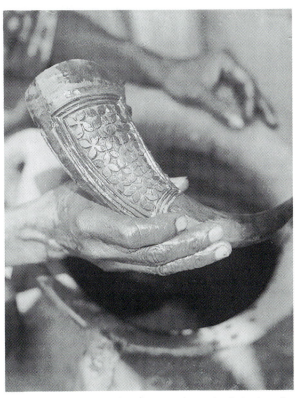

15   The horn must be frequently soaked during the process of carving.

16   The three symbols: double gong, cowrie shells, and lizard, Babungo-Mbuakang, January 1992

17 The symbol of the frog, Babungo-Mbuakang,
January 1992

18 The full figure of a nobleman, Babungo-
Mbuakang, January 1992

19 The combination of the symbols of earth
spider and cowrie shell, Bali-Nyonga, November
1991

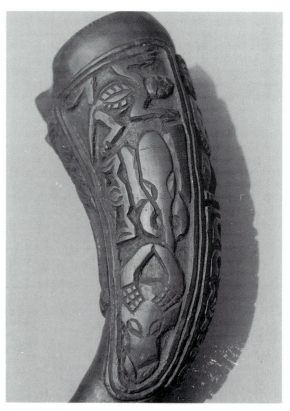

20 The combination of the three symbols of the
buffalo head, elephant head and lizard, Bamessing,
March 1990

21 The combination of the three symbols of the buffalo head, earth spider and palm tree, Bali-Nyonga, November 1991

22 The combination of the three symbols of the lizard, a nobleman's head, and the earth spider, Bali-Nyonga, November 1991

23 The symbol of the hunting net, Bali-Nyonga, May 1992

24 The combination of the symbols of the cowrie shells and the double gong, Bali-Nyonga, November 1991

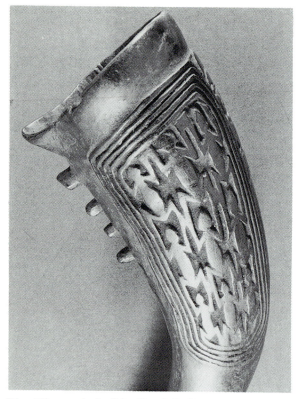

25 The symbol of the lizard, Bali-Nyonga, February 1990

26 A small collection of title-cups, Bali-Nyonga, November 1991

27 The black cap worn by members of *ngumba*, Bali-Nyonga, November 1992

28 A drinking cup carved in Foumban, March 1993

LOST-WAX CASTING

Lost-wax casting is an art practised widely across sub-Saharan West Africa, an art of savanna and forest, of centralised courts and stateless societies, of elites and commoners. For a thousand years and more, casters have produced masterpieces in copper and copper alloys, from the life-sized heads of ancient Ife to the miniature gold weights of the Akan. If the metal arts of Ife and Benin and of the Akan have tended in the past to overshadow all else, casting traditions in other parts of the sub-continent are at least beginning to receive the attention they deserve. Among these is the brass-casting industry of the Cameroon Grasslands, the southernmost extension of lost-wax casting in Africa.   (Herbert, 1990:69)

Lost-wax casting as practised in Bamoum has been well documented in Herbert (1990), and in Bali-Nyonga by Fröhlich (1979).

This chapter records my observations of this particular art of brass-casting at Nkwen-Bamenda first, and then at Foumban over more than three decades. But of more value than these observations was my personal experience during the period when we were compelled by circumstances to open and run our own casting workshop in the Prescraft Centre at Bali-Nyonga in 1977 (1). I gained an even more profound insight in 1990 through a five-month trial and experimentation period at Prespot Bamessing with Prescraft ex-trainee Linus Gwanmesia (19), native of Bali-Nyonga, followed by the expert assistance from master caster Emmanuel Che (11), native of Bafut, who is also an ex-trainee of Prescraft Bali-Nyonga.

THE TECHNIQUE OF BRASS CASTING IN LOST WAX

The first step is to form the object to be cast in beeswax (2, 3). The cast metal will later take precisely the form of the wax model; hence the name 'lost-wax'.

For modelling, a big lump of beeswax is warmed by a fire (4) or a burning lamp. Small pieces are peeled off and rubbed between the thumb and the index finger to make it soft and malleable. Such a piece may be shaped between the fingers or with a soft piece of wood tapered at both ends. The sculptor constantly moistens the stick with his tongue to keep the wax from sticking while designing. (5)

Small objects are modelled of solid wax (2, 3). Larger or hollow ones such as bells, pipe-bowls, flower vases, big animals or hollow bracelets are shaped around a previously made and dried clay core (6). This is done to avoid using too much brass and to keep down the weight of the finished article.

When the wax model is completed, it is sealed first with one layer of fine, airless, wet earth following every outline of the model (7), making sure it is airtight. With small objects a clay projection must be added to each model (8) to provide anchorage for the inlet stick. Before the first layer is fully dry, the inlet sticks are inserted. When the first layer is completely dry, a second layer of somewhat coarser clay is added to the first one (9). This dual coating takes the precise imprint of the wax model and at the same time is able to withstand the heat of the furnace and the pressure of the molten metal during casting.

Often several models are enclosed in one single mould (10, 11, 12).

Usually casting is done in a single cycle, i.e. the wax model and the metal required are packed in one and the same mould. A funnel-shaped crucible is formed on top of the mould containing the wax (11, 12) with a hole or holes in the centre leading to the wax model. When the clay added to form the crucible is dry, the inlet sticks are removed so that the inlet channels leading to the wax models are now free (13). This funnel forms part of the crucible itself and is filled with small broken pieces of scrap metal (14). Only experience teaches the proper quantity of metal to use: too much might cause the mould to burst. The metal is first covered with paper in order to stop particles of earth entering the crucible and then closed up with a special mixture of earth and horse dung which is extremely heat-resistant. The crucible on top of the mould then looks like a ball about the size of a big grapefruit (15). The completed mould is dried in the sun (16) or over the fire.

When about a dozen moulds are ready, the furnace is prepared. It consists of a protecting half-wall with a semi-circular wall in front of it. At each firing, the semi-circular wall is re-built. When this has been done the moulds are carefully set in charcoal with the crucible facing down (17).

Hidden behind the half-wall of the furnace, on the floor, is a pair of hand-bellows. The bellows blow air through metal or clay tubes to increase the temperature. They are made of the inner tube of a car tyre stretched over wooden bowls. Once the charcoal fire is burning, the operator puts his thumbs through the loops in the middle of the two rubber sheets, and sets up a drum-like rhythm (18).

Extra charcoal is added, a handful at a time, all around the moulds, filling in spaces between them and the furnace wall. In all, three charges of charcoal are added in the course of the five-hour firing, but only gradually to avoid too rapid a rise in temperature. Occasional cracks in the furnace are filled with mud to seal it as much as possible and in order to maintain the required temperature. The top of the furnace is covered with iron sheets under a layer of charcoal in order to add heat from above (19). The slow build-up of heat drives any possible moisture out of the moulds and melts the wax before the temperature is hot enough to melt the metal. The melted wax is absorbed in the porous coating.

It is of importance that the fire is constantly controlled, which is to say, the caster must make sure that the fire surrounds each and every mould equally and the heat must be maintained and provide an even temperature all round (20). When the temperature reaches about 1000 °C inside the moulds, the metal melts. It is a matter of practice and experience to know the right time to remove the moulds from the furnace. The experienced caster knows that the metal has melted by a number of signs:

- all charcoal has been burnt;
- there is no longer any smoke;
- light greenish-coloured vapour appears around each mould;
- the vapour is accompanied by sparks.

Before further action, the caster must also make sure that the upper part of each mould has reached the same high temperature, for it is possible that the crucible low down in the charcoal fire has reached the required temperature while the upper part of the mould is still 'cold' (21). If so, the casting cannot be successful. The whole mould must show a uniform red-hot colour.

The caster grasps and removes the first mould from the furnace with a pair of raphia tongs (22). At this point, the crucible is still in the downward position. While holding the mould with the pair of tongs with his two hands, he shakes it vigorously, turns it upside down and puts it gently to one side (22). The melted metal runs straight through the channels into the hollow mould. The caster repeats this with one mould after another, lining them up on the floor until the furnace is empty. The pair of tongs is a simple, home-made instrument, a piece of a split raphia stem folded over in the middle. Before use its ends are soaked in water. When turning the moulds upside down, it may happen that one mould has a crack through which the melted metal gushes out. The caster is prepared for such eventualities. He swiftly takes a bit of wet earth and smears it over the damaged spot with his bare thumb (23).

The moulds are cooled with water (24) and the tops of the crucibles knocked off. The superfluous metal cake which is still red hot is lifted out with a file handle (25) and immediately broken into smaller pieces on the floor (26) for ease of use next time. The moulds are again sprinkled with water and then broken open (27).

When the cast objects have cooled, the caster breaks off the brass rod, or runner, formed by the inlet hole and files off any unwanted rough edges and spikes. A well-cast piece has no roughness on the surface and is even in colour. The castings may simply be polished or they may be coloured golden brown or black (28).

LEARNING FROM EXPERIENCE

At the beginning of 1977, a new section was added to the Prescraft Production Centre at Bali-Nyonga: lost-wax casting. The sole reason for opening a brass-casting section was the urgent need for castings of good quality. As far back as 1961 the Presbyterian Handicraft Centre (Prescraft) got their brass articles from the brass-casters at Nkwen-Bamenda.

Under the influence of tourism their quality gradually declined, so that we decided to start our own brass production. The business prospered until 1990 when, owing to changes in the Prescraft management and other occurrences, there was an acute shortage of staff. The only ex-trainee left, Linus Gwanmesia, was not experienced enough to carry on successfully on his own. He joined me in Bamessing where he installed his casting workshop within the campus of the pottery project. Between May and September 1990, he made four trial castings each time with 11 or 12 moulds in the furnace. Most of the moulds contained four to seven wax models. Thanks to detailed recording each time from the beginning to the end, it was possible to learn from the failures and correct the errors of every preceding casting.

Though the caster had achieved a considerable improvement by the time of the third trial, the quality of 'our' castings (29) was no better than that produced by the Nkwen casters. Since the two of us were at our wits' end, we decided to seek expert advice from the Prescraft ex-trainee, Emmanuel Che, working independently at Upper Bayelle-Bamenda. His expertise so impressed me that there and then we agreed that 'my' caster would take an additional three-month crash course under his supervision. The training agreed upon was carried out and paid its dividends.

I give here a summary of what I personally learned from the whole exercise. For me the following points are the secret of good casting.

- The special quality of earth used for coating the wax models and for forming the mould and the attached crucible is of the utmost importance. Whenever casters talk about the type of earth, or earth-mixture (30), with which they work they always say that it must be 'powerful'.

'Powerful' here means: earth that does not crack in the fire. Maybe 'heat-resistant' would be the right term. Several types of clay which are used in the making of pots were tested at Bamessing for coating wax models and forming moulds and crucibles. The pottery clay proved to be 'powerful' but it was almost impossible to remove the fired clay from the castings. For this reason pottery-clay had to be abandoned for casting purposes. Moreover we found that earth containing iron oxide is not suitable for it does not withstand the pressure.

- Mixing earth and horse dung. Once the right earth is known it must be mixed with organic matter, such as horse dung. But horse dung also comes in different types: rough or smooth depending on what the horse is fed on. The dung must be fresh. In the absence of a fresh supply our man in Bamenda uses undigested grass removed from the intestines of slaughtered cows, collecting it very early in the morning from the slaughterhouse. However, fresh horse dung is best; better still is fresh donkey dung, though this is difficult to get.

- The next problem is knowing the proper proportions of earth and horse dung to use. The first thing to be done is to break open the horse droppings and check whether the dung is rough or smooth since its quality determines the proportion of earth to dung. If the horse dung is rough a lesser quantity is taken than in the case of smooth dung. Rough dung results from rough feed. For instance in the dry season the feed is dry and tough whereas in the wet season it is fresh and tender.

- Two different mixtures are then prepared: one for the first coat of the wax models, and one for the second and third coats. For the first coat, both earth and horse dung must be sifted. The two elements are mixed, then water added and kneaded thoroughly. After kneading, a lump is made and broken to see whether or not the mixture is good. If not, either ingredient is added as required. For the second and third coatings unsifted earth and dung are mixed. In this mixture the proportion of dung is higher than in the one for the first coat. Again water is added and the mass kneaded. Since the earth as well as the dung differ in quality every time, one cannot just follow a standard recipe. The right proportions can only be known from experience.

- The mixtures are left to 'rest' for two weeks. During this time it will turn into a smooth, sticky mass. In this condition it is ready to be used for coating and forming the mould and the funnel-shaped crucible attached to the mould.

- After the metal pieces have been placed in the crucible, a special mixture of the best, meaning the most 'powerful', unsifted earth, mixed with about the same amount of unsifted horse dung must be made and used for closing up the crucible. This last step is most important.

- All the experiments made with ingredients other than horse or donkey dung, such as sawdust, wood ash, antelope hair, charcoal dust, or cow dung proved to be possible, yet the best results were achieved with horse and donkey dung.

- If the sticks to make the channels leading from the metal chamber (crucible) to the wax model are not placed with the utmost care, the result will be a defective casting. The sticks made of the bark of the raphia leaf-stem should be of the thickness of a pencil. The pointed end must be set deep into the wax model. In the case of a thin-walled wax model, extra wax has to be added at the spot where the stick enters the model, so that it can be set deeply enough into the wax. After casting, such a thickening has to be filed down.

- When moulding the wax models, details, such as eyes, mouths, feet, hands and so on must be marked distinctly and deeply, so that they are shown clearly in the negative and in the cast object respectively.

- When setting the moulds in the furnace, the gaps between the moulds must be blocked with pieces of previously fired, broken moulds. If this is not done, the air blown into the furnace by the bellows will just pass upwards without being forced to spread and reach the utmost front of the furnace. The result is that the moulds in the foremost row remain 'cold', an experience we had in the second trial casting.

- The quality of the metal used is also of great significance. Brass, an alloy of copper and zinc, is an ideal metal for casting since it has a relatively low melting-point and flows evenly. The raw material was imported though not for the purpose of brass-casting. There were two brass currencies in circulation in this region. Elderly informants say that up to the end of World War II brass spirals (31) were used as money, especially to pay for valuable 'things', such as women. Up to 100 spirals for a pretty woman was common. They further reveal that besides Dane guns, black gunpowder, cloths, salt and beads also long brass rods, 6mm thick, were shipped into Calabar by European merchants in exchange for ivory, palm oil and slaves. These rods were cut into lengths of 1m by the local traders and wound four times round a stick of 7.5cm in diameter. These spirals weighing a little over 200gm each served first of all as bangles in the Calabar region, but were soon spread as an inland currency in Southern Nigeria and Southern Cameroon, especially, along the Cross River up to Mamfe and along the long-distance trade route to Bali-Nyonga, Bamenda, Meta' and Esimbi. These same brass rods, so it is said, were also worked into manillas (31) and used as money. When I arrived in the Southern Cameroons in the mid-1950s, it was still administered as part of British Nigeria. The half-penny stamp then in circulation showed the old manilla currency which was used by both Nigeria and this part of the Cameroons (32). While the brass rods were all of the same size, the manillas were used in three different sizes representing three different values. Small items, however, were paid for in cowries (31). In pre-colonial times the means of exchange used in the Western Grasslands, such as hoes and swords made locally of wrought smelted iron, beads from Europe, cowrie shells from the Indian Ocean, brass manillas and spirals, were of much greater value than after the introduction of foreign currencies. An informant's father in Bali-Nyonga was bought as a slave for one single brass spiral whereas 25 pieces were paid for his mother not long before the turn of the century. Thereafter an ever increasing inflation of the West African currency must have taken place. There are many informants who say that their mothers were bought for 200-300 and more brass spirals at the time of World War II. After the war this means of payment gradually died out.

While manillas are hardly seen nowadays, brass spirals can still be found in practically every weekly Bali-Nyonga and Tad market, though no longer in large numbers. Just a few weeks ago I bought 100 of them from a trader in the Tad market. If bought in dozens, one may get them for CFA 200 each. Four and a half spirals make one kilogram which gives a kilogram price of CFA 900 against CFA 350 to 400 for one kilogram of scrap brass . From this it is obvious that brass spirals, if used at all, are only for special items or those that fetch a good price. These brass spirals have been in great demand ever since brass-casting was started in Foumban at the beginning of this century, in Nkwen-Bamenda in 1946 and in Bali-Nyonga in 1977.

Alhaji Salifu Njikomo from Foumban (born in 1933) tells me that during World War II and thereafter, his father, being a caster, used to send him to Mankon and Meta' to buy brass spirals and have them transported to Foumban. Today casters depend on scrap brass, such as car radiators, bolts, taps, hinges, locks, cartridge cases and the like. Since such scrap brass contains different alloy mixtures, casters often complain that it is far more difficult to obtain good castings nowadays than it was in former times.

When our expert caster in Upper Bayelle-Bamenda was asked to cast a church bell 60cm in height, he did not join the crucible to the mould but melted the metal in a separate vessel. From this he poured the melted metal into the pre-heated mould. Moreover, if he has to cast small items, such as clappers for bells, finger rings and such like, he prepares the moulds without an attached crucible. In this case, he puts surplus metal into one or more crucibles to which a wax model in its mould is attached. When removing the mould from the furnace with the crucible still facing down, he puts the mould gently on the floor. Holding the mould with the tongs in his left hand and slanting it backwards, he pierces a hole in the crucible with a file handle using his right hand. He pours some of the melted brass into the other ready-made and heated mould which has no crucible of its own. He then turns the mould in his left hand upside down in order to allow the melted metal to run into its own form.

There is a half life-sized figure of a horse in Alhaji Salifu Njikomo's outer court in Foumban that has been cast in eight pieces and afterwards welded together.

Staple products made by the lost-wax process are:

bells (33), gongs (34) and tobacco pipes (35), (bowl and stem separately), bracelets (36), pendants, finger rings and key rings (37), masks (38) and neck rings (39), horsemen, native houses and figures of daily life (40), medical figures (41), calabash-like flower vases (42), chess figures (43) and nativity scenes (44).

Being asked about the origin and use of brass bells, Alhaji Salifu Njikomo from Foumban had this to say:

There are three types of ancient bells and one type conforming to modern ideas in style and design. The very first bell which was thinly cast, was made in Bamoum. On the outside surface there was a spotted design. The bell was provided with a clapper and a brass loop on top for easy handling or tying (45c). It was my grandfather who started making this type of bell. He made them to be hung on the war cutlasses of Bamoum warriors so that they could be heard running and fighting from afar.

The second type of bell was a rather thick casting, also provided with a tongue. The horizontal cross-section of the body was oval in shape. The surface of the body was designed with the spiral pattern below and the zigzag pattern above. On a short neck there was a large ornamented knob of openwork. It showed the pattern of two times four stylised frogs: four round the upper half of the knob and four round its lower half (45a). This bell was used in traditional courts and society meetings. If a person was found guilty, the bell was placed before them and was only removed after payment of the fine imposed. The smallest fine was one goat.

The third type of 'bell' was without a clapper, in fact what nowadays we call a gong (45b). It is held upside down and hit with a stick, just as is done with the iron gong. Such brass gongs are used for dances in the king's court only, or by the king himself or his high ranking people to call the people to the palace for a very important announcement. There is, in addition, a modern type of bell with all kinds of designs on it, such as human beings, birds, snakes, chameleons, lizards, frogs, spiders and so on (33). The creation of this bell was requested by a Basel missionary who took special interest in king Njoya's activities, (I presume it was Anna Rein-Wuhrmann, HK), my father made the first bell of this kind.

Following further detailed descriptions as to size, shape and design and a photograph shown him by Alhaji Salifu Njikomo, our caster Emmanuel Che succeeded in reproducing the three ancient types of bells as shown below (see illustration 45).

20   An even temperature all round is needed, Bamessing-Ntukwe, August 1990.

1 Casting workshop at Prescraft Bali-Nyonga, August 1980

2 Model in solid wax, height *c.* 12cm, Nkwen-Bamenda, January 1975

3 Model in solid wax, length *c.* 13cm, Prescraft Bali-Nyonga, June 1978

4 Warming the lump of beeswax, Prescraft Bali-Nyonga, September 1978. The brick sized lump of wax is on top of the semi-circular wall on the left.

5 The modelling stick must be frequently moistened, Foumban, June 1976.

6 Hollow objects need a clay core, Prescraft Bali-Nyonga, August 1980.

7 The wax model is sealed, Prescraft Bali-Nyonga, March 1977.

8 Sealed and unsealed wax models, the former showing the projection for the inlet stick, Prescraft Bali-Nyonga, April 1977

9 Wax models coated a second time and with sticks inserted to create the inlet channels, Prescraft Bali-Nyonga, March 1977

10 Several models are enclosed in one mould, Prescraft Bali-Nyonga, May 1977.

11 The funnel-shaped crucible is added, Prescraft Bali-Nyonga, May 1977, Emmanuel Che at work.

12   The funnel-shaped crucible is added, Prescraft Bali-Nyonga, May 1977.

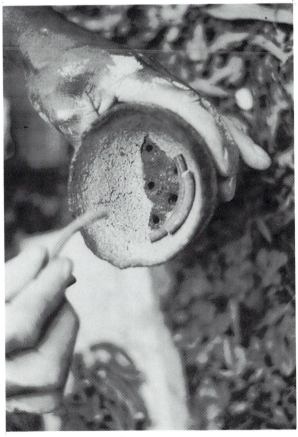

13   The sticks have been removed from the inlet channels, Prescraft Bali-Nyonga, March 1977.

14   Scrap brass is put into the crucible, Prescraft Bali-Nyonga, June 1978.

15 The closed-up crucible, Prescraft Bali-Nyonga, May 1977

16 Drying the moulds, Prescraft Bali-Nyonga, May 1978

17 The moulds in the furnace, Bamessing-Ntukwe, August 1990

18   Air is pumped into the furnace, Nkwen–Bamenda, September 1972

19   The furnace is covered with burning charcoal lying on metal sheeting, Bamessing–Ntukwe, August 1990, Linus Gwanmesia working the bellows.

Note: for illustration 20 see page 36.

21 The upper part of the moulds are still 'cold' Nkwen-Bamenda, November 1975.

22 Removing the hot moulds, Prescraft Bali-Nyonga, May 1977

23 Repairing a crack in the mould, Nkwen-Bamenda, December 1978. The caster's thumb can be seen at the bottom of the photograph.

24 Cooling the moulds, Prescraft Bali-Nyonga, May 1977

25 Lifting out the superfluous metal cake, Prescraft Bali-Nyonga, May 1977

26 Breaking up the metal cake, Prescraft Bali-Nyonga, May 1977

27 The broken mould, Nkwen-Bamenda, January 1975

28 The finished object is identical with its wax model (see 2), Nkwen-Bamenda, January 1975.

29   Object of poor quality with rough and irregular surface, height *c.* 10cm, Bamessing-Ntukwe, August 1990

30   Mixing different types of earth, Prescraft Bali–Nyonga, August 1980

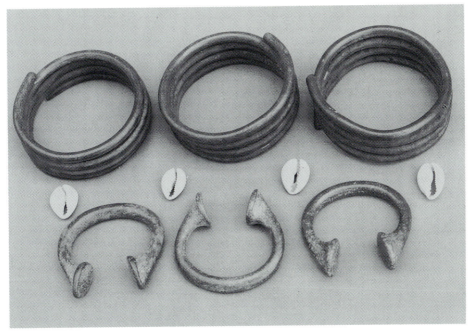

31   Brass spirals manillas and cowrie shells, Bali-Nyonga, January 1993

32   Colonial half-penny stamp, Fotabe, November 1956

33   Modern type of bell, height *c.* 15cm, Nkwen–Bamenda, March 1971

34   Brass cast gong, height *c.* 20cm, Nkwen–Bamenda, July 1971

35   Brass tobacco pipe, total length 51cm (head front 20cm, cast perforated stem 19cm, thin copper pipe 18cm), Nkwen–Bamenda, March 1971

36   Brass bracelets, Bamessing-Ntukwe, September 1990

37   Brass pendants and a finger-ring, Bamessing-Ntukwe, August 1990

38   Model face-mask in brass, total height 27cm, Bali-Nyonga, May 1992

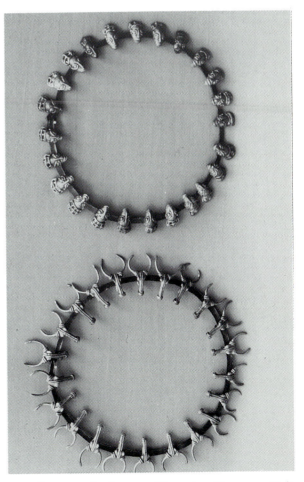

39   Brass neck-rings *c.* 32cm in diameter, Bali-Nyonga, October 1992

40 Brass figures of daily life, Prescraft Bali-Nyonga, April 1978

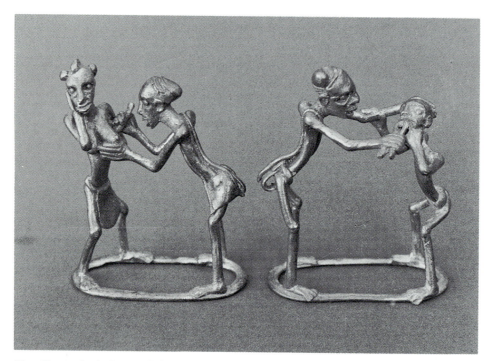

41 Brass depictions of the work of traditional doctors, Prescraft Bali-Nyonga, November 1992

42   Brass calabash-like flower vase, height *c.* 18cm,
Prescraft Bali-Nyonga, November 1992

43   Brass chess figures, Prescraft Bali-Nyonga, March 1976

44   Brass crib scene, Bamessing-Ntukwe, August 1990

45a–c (from left to right)   Copies (a and c) of ancient brass bells, height 19cm, and (b) a gong, height 28cm, Bali-Nyonga, November 1992

TRADITIONAL POTTERY

Everyday pottery was produced more or less everywhere in the Western Grasslands. Basic earthenware vessels were made for different uses and functions and were therefore of different sizes and kinds, such as large *mimbo* pots, *mimbo* jugs, pots for brewing corn-beer, large pots for water-storage, big and small cooking pots and soup bowls. All these objects were made appropriate for ordinary, everyday use and had to be strong and durable, but were almost devoid of decoration (1).

Some chiefdoms, especially on the Ndop Plain, specialised in the manufacture of artistic earthenware, namely Bamessing (Nsei), Babessi and Babungo; Bamessing taking pre-eminence among the three potter villages.

It is surprising how well the potter's trade has survived in Bamessing in these changing times, when, in many parts of Africa and particularly in Cameroon, the traditional arts and crafts are dying out. But there is no doubt that Bamessing pottery has also undergone obvious changes in the course of time. Certain old types of tobacco pipes, for instance, or ingeniously and skilfully decorated soup and oil pots are no longer produced. Also many formerly graceful and well-proportioned forms have given way to heavier and unwieldy ones. New earthenware has been developed, especially since the early seventies, which is made mainly for tourists. There is now a whole range of such earthenware souvenirs, some of them bearing the inscription 'Greetings from Cameroon'. Among them are Cameroonian soldiers and gendarmes, the state president and ministers, traditional dignitaries, pastors, elders, and Christian Women's Fellowship members, all in their uniforms and colourfully painted (2), but also animals, such as golden lions (3), dogs etc. While its aesthetic quality has been questioned, it remains an important source of livelihood.

One clever innovation was the production of trophies, cups for football, handball, volleyball, and many other competitions - coloured silver and gold. Apparently they sell well. I had been keenly observing this development since January 1961 when I was put in charge of church schools

and congregations in the then Bafut-Ndop church district. I was able to combine this comprehensive task with the initiation of the handicraft scheme which, ten years later, resulted in an independent enterprise, known today as Prescraft. Before settling in Bamessing in 1983, I had been a frequent visitor to the village throughout the 1960s and 1970s, either alone for business or with interested tourists who were numerous in those days. Whenever I went on home-leave, I used to visit the Cameroon art collections in European museums where I discovered many a design, be it woodwork, pottery or some other craft, already forgotten in Cameroon. Each time I came back with a collection of photographs, took them to the respective craftsmen and discussed ways and means of reviving the designs, following the photographs with their given measurements. Thus old designs were re-introduced, in some cases slightly modified to match the present time.

In the Mbeghang-Bamessing quarter I worked first with Fomba Africa on various types of soup bowls, especially those with perforated pedestals, two handles and a lid, called *kuebeko* (4), and also on the famous tobacco bowls (5) for which his skill was already renowned. My keen interest in his craft, my furnishing him with 'new' ideas (at times still remembered by him), as well as being a potential buyer, developed into a real friendship with him and the entire family, which of course became even stronger during the time when I became a neighbour of his in the 1980s. It was a hard blow to the whole quarter when Fomba Africa, not yet an old man, passed away in September 1989.

The second potter with whom I worked was Ngang Hans, also residing in the Mbeghang quarter, just a short distance farther up the hill beyond Fomba Africa's residence. His soup bowls (*kuebeto*) which have neither pedestal nor lid, but a handle and a spout instead, are of a slightly different style but meticulously decorated with geometrical designs, either carved or impressed.

The third and fourth male potters who repeatedly and successfully copied old pipebowls were Keh Bamessing Keh, and Keh Bamenda

Gweh. There is no doubt that these four potters were the leading lights of Bamessing pottery in the 1960s, and still were 20 years later when I began to work with the entire Bamessing potters' guild even more closely and intensely.

The best women potters – who by 'tradition' are confined to the production of cooking pots, frying pans, water storage pots and the like are: Magdalene Ngwe, the wife of master potter Keh Bamessing Keh; Theresia Begha, the daughter of master potter Ngang Hans; Mary Fomba, the wife of master potter Fomba Africa; Theresia Nobane, and Esther Mbo. All of them come from Mbeghang quarter, except Esther Mbo, the daughter of Theresia Nobane from Mbesoh quarter because she married someone from that quarter.

Peculiar to the Nsei pottery is the phenomenon that the potter's trade is practised by artisans of both sexes. This is well known to ethnologists who have studied and written about Nsei pottery. The general consensus in the literature is that there is a strict division of labour between male and female potters. It is said that women exclusively make simple cooking pots while men, just as exclusively, make figurative products.

I agree that, generalising and simplifying, one can say that women produce the simple household commodities and the men the more artistic and sophisticated objects. But it is equally true that many a woman has the skill to make beautifully designed vessels, and many men know nothing other than making the ordinary everyday cooking pots. However, a strict division of labour does indeed exist when it comes to the production of vessels exclusively used by men, more especially by dignitaries, nobles and secret societies, or in *Manjong* Houses. Traditionally, such objects are made by men only. It must be made evident that this dividing line is not so much determined by the work involved, but by the use and user of the object. The women potters are not less gifted than the men.

Not all pots made by men show applied figurative designs (6). Women are able and permitted to make everything in pottery that men make. The only restriction on women is when it comes to objects meant to be used only by men or by men's societies.

It is possible to imagine two mimbo pots which are very much alike, one made by a man, the other by a woman. In this case both pots have rolled or impressed designs and are intended for ordinary use. Supposing the very same type of mimbo pot is needed for a men's society, it must be made by a male potter and show applied figurative ornament.

Bamessing is famous for its unique figurative pipebowls of remarkable aesthetic value. The pipemakers were all male artists. Old pipes reveal exquisite design and workmanship on the clay bowls as well as on the wooden or ivory stems (7,8,9). In most cases it was the same craftsmen who carried out the work, revealing the great variety of traditional symbols whether human or animal figures, geometrical patterns, or a mixture of both. There can be no doubt that the tobacco pipe was a prestige object and a clear indicator of the rank and title of the owner in society (10). The commoner had his plain or moderately decorated pipe. Giant ceremonial pipes were reserved for use by the *Fon* when needed on public occasions.

The woman's tobacco pipe is rather different. It is noteworthy that the small plain or simply decorated pipebowl used by women was made by the women themselves. Very often the stem was nothing else than a thin smooth stem of Indian bamboo (11).

Though Bamessing has long been known for the production of clay pipes *par excellence*, they were also made in other places, for instance at Babungo. The masterpieces, however, originate from Bamessing though in the literature they erroneously go under the name, 'Bali pipes'. This error dates back to the turn of the century when these tobacco pipes were collected, packed and sent to Germany via the then German colonial Grassland Headquarters in Bali-Nyonga.

A speciality peculiar to the Western Grasslands, most probably to one of the Ndop Plain potter villages, is the face-masks made of clay, said to be unique. But the production of these masks was discontinued long ago because of their fragility.

Bamessing potter's lore has been handed down from generation to generation over the centuries. It is naturally taught to children by their parents, from father to son, from mother to daughter, and one neighbour freely learns it from another. If a girl, who is a potter, is married to a man from another quarter (as happened with Esther Mbo), interested persons may learn the trade from her free of charge. But many potter-girls who marry outside their quarter, give the trade up if the clay is at too great a distance. (The farthest Bamessing quarters, Mufuo I and Mufuo II, are between 7-10km away from the clay source.) That is why pottery is practised only in those quarters which are near the clay source at Ntukwe, namely: Mbesoh (3km), Mbeghang (2km) and Ntukwe, itself (½-1km).

In one single case a man from Akum (Santa) was trained by Fomba Africa for a period of nine months for which he paid the sum of CFA 15,000 which included board and lodging.

The Bamessing traditional potters work to a fixed eight day rhythm (the traditional week) thus:

Day One, *Wigha*: digging of the clay at the clay source, in Ntukwe quarter, just enough for the week's work, and transportation of the wet clay to their compounds by head-load. The women especially do this part of the work, in small groups, between two and five people, though afterwards they work independently. On the same day the two different types of clay are mixed together, pounded and finally a certain amount of river sand is added in order to get the desired quality.

Day Two, *Kwodiah*: forming and moulding;

Day Three, *Wintukwe*: forming and moulding;

Day Four, *Witieh*: forming and moulding, drying;

Day Five, *Ketembu*: moulding, dressing, decorating, burnishing, drying;

Day Six, *Kweleh*: finishing touches, rubbing with *engobe*, burnishing, drying and firing, sale at the door;

Day Seven, *Wingang*: Bamessing market day: sale of the products;

Day Eight, *Winkoh*: traditional 'Sunday'.

THE PREPARATION OF THE CLAY

The preparation of the clay is an amazingly short process. Usually two types of clay are mixed together with sand. In order to cut the clay, a dark-grey, at times even a black type of clay is mixed with a brownish-reddish type which contains muck and coarse quartz-sand. Both types of clay are found along either river bank almost at the end of the western quarter of Ntukwe. The excavation of the clay and its transport home is usually done in small groups of two to five potters (13) because it is a hard and dangerous task. The clay is mined in pits and at times in tunnels. To get the wet clay out and to deposit it on a terrace is hard labour which requires more than one person (12). It has happened that a potter mining clay alone in a pit or, most especially, in a tunnel was digging his own grave.

The two heaps of clay will be measured out into miners' baskets, plastic or enamel containers. Each forms a headload that can weigh as much as a bag of cement. At home each potter works independently in his or her compound. The two types of clay are thrown into one heap and the mixture is not made to the same proportions every time but is decided upon intuitively according to the nature and quality of that day's clay. The same applies to the question of whether sand must be added, and if so, in what quantity. Having made the clay into a heap, the next thing to be done is to chop the clay lumps into small pieces. The men usually use a cutlass, the women a hoe. In the process, coarse impurities are removed (14) and sometimes some river sand is added to the clay.

By means of a long heavy wooden pestle, the mixture is processed, either on a wooden plank, or a large concave stone; sometimes a grinding stone is used (15) and the clay is pounded to the required consistency and malleability. This too is a refining process during which stones, roots and any other coarse particles in the clay are removed. It takes approximately one hour to prepare enough clay for a day's work. A thin clay has a lower percentage of shrinkage and subsequently is less likely to crack when dried and baked.

FORMING AND MOULDING

There are two techniques of forming and moulding in Bamessing pot-making. One may be called the 'lump' or 'pulling' method and the other the 'coil' method (similar to coiling a basket).

The 'Lump' Method

An example is the lady potter, Theresia Nobane, of the Mbeghang quarter making a series of cooking pots. First of all she fetches a good number of large cocoyam leaves. She puts two of them cross-wise on top of each other on the ground and takes a lump of the ready-made clay which she rolls into a long thick python-like coil on a wooden board (16). With the palms of her hands she beats the coil into a wide flat strip. Taking it up and transferring it over to the cocoyam leaves, she bends it round, placing it in a circular form on the leaves and joins the two ends together (17). In a stooping position, Theresia Nobane now pulls the thick clay strip out to become wider and thinner thus forming the umbrella-like bottom of the pot between the fingers of her right and the palm of her left hand ensuring an equal thickness throughout (18).

While the completed bottom part is left to dry in the sun, the potter goes on to repeat this process again and again up to ten times a day. After a few hours she comes back to the first piece to continue her work on it. Having scraped the surface with a piece of a broken calabash or the like, smoothed and burnished it with a flat stone, the bottom part is turned over and set into a *kata*, a wreath-like ring which is made by winding round dry banana or plantain leaves. In the case of a large pot, the bottom part has to stay untouched for a night or so.

The upper portion is made in the same way as the bottom part (19). A thick, wide clay band is worked onto the mouth of the bottom part and again pulled up. The pot gradually grows into shape under the pressure and counter-pressure of two brisk and lively hands. She scrapes and smooths over the inner and outer surfaces from time to time. Having reached this upper stage of the process, the bellied-out wall is now drawn in with every step the potter takes, moving backwards round the pot (20), narrowing it into a short yet wide neck. All that now remains to be done is the curling out of the top circular edge to form the rim or lip.

With a wetted tree-leaf in the right hand, the potter, pinching the soft, malleable clay rim, gently moves two to three times round the pot (21). The rim and its edge are now perfectly round and smooth. When the rim is slightly dry and stiff, the potter takes the leather-hard pot on her left thigh with her left hand. She must hold it from the inside to support it while she taps on the wall of the vessel with a wooden block in her right hand over the entire wall area to even out its thickness (22). This is an exercise of the utmost importance.

Under the neck of the completed cooking pot, either a short piece (3-4cm) of twisted fibre-twine or an empty maize cob is rolled over the soft surface leaving behind a subdued decoration on what is otherwise a cheap, plain cooking pot. From a half calabash or a broken pot, a slip of miceous earth (ochre) of a pale yellowish-brown colour is rubbed over the entire pot's surface both inside and out. When dried the surface is burnished with a piece of metal or a smooth pebble. A pot thus treated acquires a silky sheen which glitters in the sun.

The completed pot is left to dry in a safe place in the house, something that can be a real problem because of wandering domestic animals, such as fowls, dogs, goats and pigs.

The earth used for colouring the pot yellowish-brown is found in small holes among the shrubs in the Mbeghang quarter.

The 'Coil' Method

The similarity between the 'coil' and the 'lump' method is self-evident. The process similarly begins with a lump of clay being placed on cocoyam leaves, which are not put on the level ground, but into a concave mould, be it a grinding stone or an old, broken pot. Whereas in the 'lump' method the bottom is formed as a convex shape, the 'coil' method starts by making the bottom concave but is later turned upside down and left to dry for a few hours. It is then returned to its former position and one long clay coil after the other is added and worked onto it to form a continuous circular shape of the desired shape and size. Cooking pots of this type are made in different sizes every week by the hundred.

The tools a Bamessing woman uses to make a cooking pot are few and simple: a flat or concave base (board, stone) two cocoyam leaves on which to work the pot, a *kata* (leaf-wreath) to keep the pot in position, a few fragments of broken calabash for scraping and burnishing, as well as a pebble to burnish the surfaces, a tree leaf or two to finalise the forming and smoothing of the brim, a small wooden block to tap the wall, and above all - her two able hands.

It may be recalled that the potter's wheel is unknown in traditional Bamessing - as it is unknown everywhere on the continent south of the Sahara. Instead of raising up the piece being worked and rotating it to enable the potter to work while stationary, it is the potter that gently moves around it in a stooping posture, in the same way that men clear the farm with their machetes and the women till the soil with their short-handled hoes.

PRESTIGE VESSELS

According to tradition, prestige vessels, which are exclusively used by men and men's societies, can only be made by men. Such *mimbo* pots, *mimbo* jars and soup bowls each bear at least one of the widespread prestige designs - above all the human head and human figure (23), reptiles, spider (24) royal animals' heads and the double gong (25). (See the chapter on Title Cups for the meanings of these images.) There are a number of male potters who are renowned in this field, especially for their exquisite workmanship and designs. They have been named above. Where prestige vessels are concerned, one other name must be added, that of James Tifung.

The speciality of the late Fomba Africa was the unique soup bowl with lid, pedestal and two handles (*kuebeko*) (4, 26). Such bowls were always made in a series of at least ten and by a mixture of the two basic methods to which he added a third - beating, carving, followed by impressing and burnishing. He had a series of modelling tools, mostly metal of which some were just old bicycle parts, whereas others had been made by Babungo

blacksmiths (26). During the modelling these tools were frequently dipped in red oil (palm oil), especially when making impressed designs or sculpting applied figurative ornaments (human heads, animal heads) or the two handles, and also when burnishing the rich and diverse geometrical patterns all over the outer surface including pedestal and lid. Fomba Africa made the highest form of prestige soup bowl, a vessel which, in the past, could only be owned and used by holders of high office. Since that time, the role of the soup bowl has changed.

In the 1960s, traders used to struggle to buy Fomba Africa's bowls, and they were on sale in Cameroonian towns as far away as Douala and Yaoundé. Fomba Africa never had to have his products transported to the weekly Bamessing market for sale. The traders came to his door to buy and collect them.

But it would be wrong to forget the various other types of soup bowls which were made and used in Bamessing and Babessi, for example the beautiful soup bowls which were lighter and more graceful but more fragile than Fomba Africa's *kuebeko*. These consist of a bowl with or without spout, with or without lid, with a pedestal, and with only one handle (27). Yet another type, the more common one, is the *kuebeto* in the form of a bowl, sometimes with, sometimes without spout and handle, but no pedestal and no lid (28). The latter type can still be seen in certain houses at Bamessing. All those soup bowls with one handle were usually kept pegged to the kitchen wall (29). Occasionally I have met an old man using this kind of object as a soup bowl, such as in 1992, when I met Helep Akeh and Ba Febele, both in Ntukwe quarter.

Both types of soup bowls (*kuebeko* and *kuebeto*) are well represented in the relatively rich and well preserved collection of terracotta objects, most especially from the Ndop region, in the Provincial Museum at Bamenda.

Kuebeko

Kuebeto

According to Paul Gebauer (1979: 267,. pls 140, 141) soup bowls have a dual purpose, namely as 'relish bowls' and/or 'night lamps'. During my stay in Bamessing and my extensive work in the Ndop Plain, I could find no evidence to confirm this. Bearing in mind the high degree of respect with which soup bowls used to be handled and reserved exclusively for the use of top-ranking men, it is simply inconceivable that such a bowl should ever have served any other purpose. Such a thing would be to show contempt for sacred traditional things and this was confirmed by many informants.

However, such enquiries revealed oil lamps which must have been used and produced in Bamessing until after the end of World War II. From the late 1940s these were gradually replaced by the newly-imported hurricane lamps (first from England and France, later from West Germany followed by lamps from Hong Kong, Taiwan, Korea and China). At the time of my investigation there were still a couple of elderly potters who said that they had made these lamps for local sale and use. They usually produced them a hundred at a time, meant for long distance trade to Nigeria. I asked two potters independently to make such a lamp each from memory. The response was beyond expectation. Within a week I had two different types of earthen oil lamps: one with a semi-globular oil container (with a shallow spout) on a column base, and a second one with a globular oil container on a pedestal (30).

The first lamp was made by Keh Bamessing Keh, probably the oldest contemporary traditional potter in Bamessing. He filled the semi-globular container with red oil (palm oil), twisted a small piece of cloth into a rope wick which would be floated in the palm oil. The dry end he placed into the spout and put a small flat stone on it to keep the wick in position. This oil lamp with its column-like stand can be handled easily. The other, globular lamp was made by potter Alphons Yenji strictly following the description of his old father. It has a hole in the upper half of the globe, through which it can be filled with oil. The stopper which closes the hole is made of the pith of the raphia rhachis. The second hole is placed right on top. The wick is inserted and oil is drawn up for the protruding end, which burns to give

light. A small pair of tongs made of the skin of the raphia rhachis is needed to pull the wick up from time to time.

I was surprised to find an old oil lamp of the semi-globular type in one of the compounds in Ntenka quarter. Apart from a broken spout, it was still intact. This old piece which is said to be more than 50 years old, looked very much like the one which Keh Bamessing Keh made from memory.

My investigation further revealed that the semi-globular type of oil lamp must have been more popular than the globular one. It was, however, not possible to find out which of the two was the older. It would seem that they were in use side by side. Having seen and tested the two oil lamps, it became clear to me that they must have been confined to use inside the house. But used by whom? The traditional Grasslander's house consisted only of one room which was heated and lit by the open hearth in the centre. It seems that the use of oil lamps cannot go any further back than to the turn of the century when the first primary schools came into being. Whether or not Western influence explains its origin remains an open question. For outdoor use, as in travelling long distances in the dark, torches were in general use. The common torch was made of a bundle of split off pieces of the dry raphia rhachis about one metre in length, tied together at one end for ease of carrying.

TOBACCO PIPEBOWLS

Fomba Africa also belonged to a group of male potters who specialised in making the figurative tobacco pipebowls mentioned above. The other two potters who used to join Fomba Africa in pipemaking are Keh Bamessing Keh and Keh Bamenda Gweh. The traditional Grasslands tobacco pipe consists of a clay bowl and a wooden stem. The prestige tobacco pipe has a clay bowl of either a stylised human or animal figure and a wooden or ivory stem carved with exquisite ornamentation, for example schematised animal designs, spiders, frogs, and elephant heads. Human heads and whole human beings as well as stems with purely geometric patterns were common (7-9). The bowls of prestige tobacco pipes varied in height from about 8–20cm and the stem in length from about 30–100cm. There are far larger pipes which have never been smoked forming part of the treasure of the Grasslands palaces though they are rarely seen among other displayed insignia because of their extreme fragility. There were tobacco pipes of a simpler form for the common man (31). The bowls of these pipes were smaller and moderately decorated with lines or small humps, and the stem was shorter and plainer.

Various types of Bamessing tobacco pipes

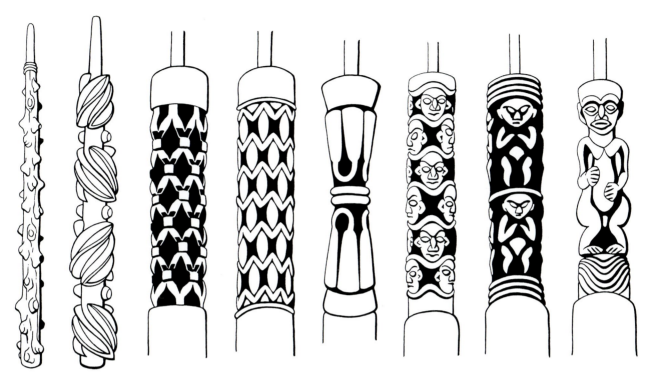

Carved wooden or ivory tobacco pipestems

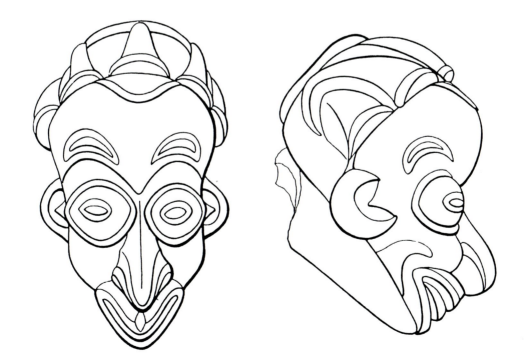

An old type of a tobacco pipehead

I often met the master potters Fomba Africa and his two elder colleagues Keh Bamessing Keh and Keh Bamenda Gweh. They liked to produce pipebowls in a batch of several dozen within a period of seven days, which is between two Bamessing market days (32).

The process of making a pipebowl 20cm high and depicting a stylised human being may be roughly and briefly described.

The potter holds a lump of plastic pipeclay in his left hand and beats it with a short piece of timber in his right, thus shaping the clay into a body resembling a truncated solid cone. Having allowed it to dry for some time, he presses and taps the facial surface with the edged piece of timber into a slightly convex shape. On either long side, a corner of the timber is depressed lengthwise into the clay and rocked sideways, which results in a sort of coil at the back side of the bowl (33). This coil is later bored out for the stem to be inserted. In the same way, the bowl is hollowed out to hold the tobacco (34). The whole pipebowl is then given its broad outlines by beating, impressing and cutting. With a small knife the artist cuts out the details such as eyes, mouth, teeth, nose, etc. and impresses the ornamental designs such as the headgear with a modelling tool (35). Having completed all the fine work, the surface is smoothed with a metallic spoon-handle, or the like, and carefully burnished.

FIRING

Every eighth day (this is always on *Kweleh*, the day prior to the Bamessing market day, *Wingang*) the sun-dried earthenware made during the week is fired. The firing is done in various places sometimes on bare, level ground or in a shallow pit, just outside the compound. The fragile sun-dried objects are laid on their sides in rows and carefully embedded between layers of dry hill grass, dry maize stalks and dry pieces of raphia rhachis of which the big ones are halved, and placed in all directions (36). They are covered with layers of twigs and again hill grass.

Traditional potters never use elephant grass stalks as fuel for firing earthenware. These have the surprising characteristic that when burnt, they do not reduce to ashes, but form into a sort of crystalline glaze which fuses with the clay objects in the fire. This always results in a damaged surface or even unpleasant holes in the clay objects when these fused crystals have to be removed.

Once the fuel heap is lit, the fire lasts no more than 15-20 minutes. I have repeatedly witnessed such brief firing times. It is obviously inadequate (37, 38) and traditional pottery in general suffers from inadequate firing. Master potter Fomba Africa and some others used a different method. They prepared the open air 'kiln' exactly in the same way as described above, but with more care than is usually taken where cooking pots are concerned. When firing his products, Fomba Africa added hardly any extra fuel as most others do, yet his firing time, with the same or even less amount of fuel, was between 45-60 minutes. How was he able to prolong the actual firing time? Once the fuel had burst into flames, he gently placed long fresh strips of the outer skin of banana and/or plantain stems on the heap thus choking and slowing down the combustion process (39). As the entire fuel was gradually reduced to ashes, the fired objects became increasingly visible. This then marked the end of the firing process.

BLACKENING

Certain small-sized earthenware objects such as soup bowls, both *kuebeto* and *kuebeko*, all sorts of pipebowls and drinking horns, are blackened in a natural way. Before they are fired, a liquid pigment is prepared. I repeatedly observed Fomba Africa doing this. He went to his raphia grove, selected and cut out half a dozen of the most mature fronds and with two tools, a coffee digger and a heavy cutlass, he dug right into the rootstock and cut the stump of the frond rhachis out, going as far down as possible. These extreme base parts of the rhachis are about 70cm long. He tied them in a bundle and carried them to his compound (40). With his cutlass he cut away the outer rough, uneven skin until the reddish, heavy pith emerged. He halved each lengthwise, having now 12 parts about 35cm long and took them to the compound's grinding stone where, with a heavy mallet, he beat each pith piece into a bundle of fibres (41). On a cross section of such a base rhachis which measured 7 x 4cm I counted 290 cellulose fibres.

Then, Fomba Africa fetched a wide basin one third full of clean water. The first loose bundle of cellulose fibres was soaked in the water and wrung out (42). This squeezed out the reddish sap they contain. The extract appeared as a concentrated dark red essence. The basin containing the liquid, together with a half calabash and a pair of tongs (which was nothing other than a half raphia rhachis bent over) were kept together in a convenient place near the open fire. Before the fuel had completely burnt to ashes, Fomba Africa took the pair of tongs and picked up a pot in the embers of the dying fire, handling the tongs with both hands. About turn! Stooping over the basin, holding the pot in his left hand, he filled the half calabash with the red essence and poured it over the hot pot. The liquid bubbled on the pot's surface instantly turning its brick red colour to black (43).

At times one can see browned rather than blackened objects. The brown colour is obtained when the extracted essence is no longer concentrated enough. This is the case when the cellulose fibres are soaked in water and wrung for a second time without adding at least some fresh fibres to the old ones. In the case of already baked but uncoloured pots, the blackening process may only result in a brownish colour when they are heated up a second time.

POTTERY AND THE ECONOMY OF BAMESSING

In February 1979, H.C. Allen carried out the work leading to his paper, 'A study of the feasibility of introducing high temperature glazed pottery production to the region of Bamenda/Bali'. Following this, I agreed to do the preliminary work for the proposed pottery project situated in Bamessing-Ntukwe. And so it happened that I spent altogether eight years and four months in Bamessing, from November 1983 to March 1988 in the Mbeghang quarter, next to the Chief's palace, and from April 1988 to March 1992 in the Ntukwe quarter. Immediately after my arrival in Bamessing, I started taking a survey of the existing pottery in the village, getting to know the Bamessing population in general and the potters in particular.

Bamessing is situated at mile 22, just over the Sabga Pass on the Ring Road east of Bamenda in the Grasslands, in the North West Province of the Republic of Cameroon. The indigenous population call this village Nsei. They form an ethnic group of their own with a population of approximately 15,000 inhabitants (1987) and a chief as their head. The Bamessing people originate from an area called Kime in Ndobo. They belong to the Tikar ethnic group and are said to have left the area because they feared the Fulani wars. When they left Kime as a family of 12, they had no special leader. Because of this question of leadership the family separated. Seven out of the 12 children with their families elected Funkoh as their leader and he led his faction to what is now Bamessing and established his Chiefdom. The first palace was built in the area called Ntukwe, about half a mile to the west of the present palace. It was the 19th Chief, Lufung Kwellah, who transferred the palace to the present site. While I lived in Bamessing, the Chief was Martin Lufung II who took over the throne in 1954 and died in 1995. He was the 28th chief in the family lineage. Bamessing is made up of 19 quarters, including the Fulanis whose settlements are scattered on the surrounding hills.

The survey on the Bamessing pottery aimed to investigate:
- the man-power currently engaged in pottery;
- their location in the chiefdom;
- the social context of production;
- the output of a potter, or a unit of potters from one market day to the next;
- identification of consumers and prices;
- estimated average income through the sale of pottery products per week.

1 The Manpower Engaged in Pottery (1983-4)

Quarter	Men	Women	Children	Total
Mbeghang				125
part-time	11	62	31	
full-time	17	4		
Total	28	66		
Ntukwe				25
part-time	3	22	–	
full-time	–	–		
Total	3	22		
Mbesoh				6
part-time	1	4	–	
full-time	–	1		
Total	1	5		
Traders*				18
Total				174

* Traders: Out of 18 traders, 14 are full-time traders. They do not trade exclusively in pottery but in other handicraft articles as well, such as the well-known woven fibre bags, knives and baskets. They are all natives of Bamessing.

2 Location in the Chiefdom

Potters are found in three quarters of the chiefdom, namely 124 in Mbeghang, 25 in Ntukwe and 7 in Mbesoh. The 18 traders are all natives of Bamessing and come from many different quarters.

3 Social Context of Production

In Mbeghang quarter 118 potters work in 32 groups with 2 to 11 people in each group and 6 potters work individually. In Ntukwe quarter, 14 potters work in 6 groups with 2 to 4 people in each group and 11 potters work individually. In Mbesoh quarter, 7 potters work in 2 groups of 3 and 4 people.

4 Output

The number of pieces a potter can produce within the given time depends on:
* whether the person is a full-time or a part-time potter;
* the type and size of the object;
* the degree of the artistic design on the object.

Consequently there is wide variation from 1 to 100 pieces a week.

5 Consumers

Out of the 156 potters, 25 work on commission only, namely 5 women, 14 men and 6 children. The orders come in weekly through traders. Such ordered articles are not taken to the Bamessing market and displayed there but are collected by the traders from the producers' compounds. The rest of the potters have their products carried as head loads to the weekly Bamessing market (44) where most of the articles are again bought by traders.

On his way from Bamessing to Widikum Kwebele Mbuta, a pottery trader from Bamessing-Ntenka would call on us at the Prescraft Centre at Bali-Nyonga at regular intervals of six to eight weeks. He did so as far back as to the 1960s, and he still does it now in the 1990s. He carries by head load the usual six large, well-made pots packed in a long basket called *kenja*. Whether loaded or unloaded he would not use a truck. He travels over 100km to Widikum on foot and the same distance back (45), this time loaded with a number of 4-gallon tins containing palm oil.

6 Average Income

The estimated average weekly income in the Bamessing Chiefdom derived from the sale of earthenware must be in the region of CFA 200,000. During the planting and harvesting seasons the proceeds may be as stated or a bit lower since there is much farm work to be done at this time. Throughout the rest of the year, however, they are considerably higher. This estimate is based on the following calculations:

22 male and female full-time potters at CFA 4,000 = 88,000

103 male and female part-time potters at CFA 1,000 = 103,000

31 children, part-time potters at CFA 500 = 15,500

Total estimated annual income 1983-4 = CFA 206,500

4 Potter Fomba Africa, Bamessing-Mbeghang, December 1983

1 Everyday pottery at the weekly market in Bamessing, February 1984

2   Clay figures at Bamessing market: Cameroon's State President Paul Biya (middle) his body guard (left) and General Simenge (right); height *c.* 21cm, February 1984

3   Clay figures at Bamessing market: lions coloured gold-bronze; height *c.* 13cm, December 1983

Note: For illustration 4 see page 65.

5   Bamessing tobacco pipeheads; height *c.* 21cm, Bamessing-Mbeghang, December 1977

6 Types of pot made by James Tifung, Bamessing-Mbeghang, December 1983

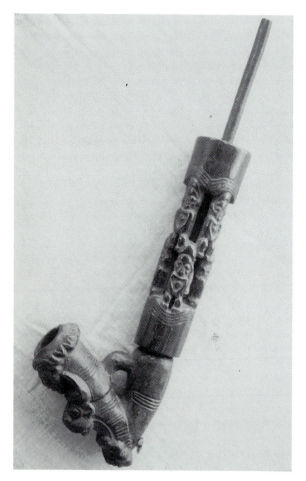

7 Old prestige tobacco pipe with carved wooden stem; length of clayhead plus carved wooden stem 27cm, owned by Gwejui Bah, Babungo-Mbuakang, April 1993

8 Old prestige tobacco pipe with carved ivory stem; length of clayhead plus carved ivory stem 31cm, owned by Gwejui Bah, Babungo-Mbuakang, April 1993

9 Old prestige tobacco pipe with carved ivory stem total length 52cm, owned by Gwejui Bah, Babungo-Mbuakang, January 1992

10 The chief of the annual dance called *nekia*, with a gang of young attendants, the *nekias*, Bamessing–Ntukwe, February 1990

11 A woman's tobacco pipe, Babungo-Ibia, December 1991

12   Mining clay, Bamessing–Ntukwe, December 1983

13   The clay is carried home, Bamessing–Ntukwe, December 1983.

14 Potter Magdalene Ngwe cutting the clay lumps, Bamessing–Mbeghang, December 1983

15 Pounding the clay on a grinding stone, Bamessing–Mbeghang, December 1983

16 Potter Theresia Nobane rolling a lump of clay into a coil, Bamessing–Mbeghang, December 1983

17   Potter Theresia Nobane forming a circle with the coil, Bamessing-Mbeghang, December 1983. A completed base is seen, inverted, on the left.

18   Potter Theresia Nobane forming an umbrella-like base, Bamessing-Mbeghang, December 1983

19   Potter Theresia Nobane adding new coils to the partly dry base, Bamessing-Mbeghang, December 1983. The base stands on a ring of dried leaves, *kata*.

20   Potter Theresia Nobane giving the pot its curved form, Bamessing–Mbeghang, December 1983

21   Potter Theresia Nobane smoothing the rim with a wetted tree-leaf, Bamessing–Mbeghang, December 1983

22   Potter Theresia Nobane tapping the wall with a wooden block, Bamessing–Mbeghang, December 1983

23 Prestige vessel decorated with human figures, height *c.* 55cm, diameter 50cm, Bamessing–Mbeghang, January 1984

24 Old palm wine pot decorated with the snake and spider motifs, height 43.5cm, diameter 44cm, Bamenda Museum, November 1983

25 Old prestige vessel of a men's society decorated with double gongs and animal heads, height 21cm, diameter 36cm, Bamenda Museum, November 1983

26 Potter Fomba Africa's locally made tools on the ground in front of his feet, Bamessing–Mbeghang, March 1984. He is working on a *kuebeko*.

27 Old soup bowls with pedestals and lids, approx. heights without handles 19.5cm, diameter 21cm, Bamenda Museum, November 1983

28 Old soup bowls without pedestals and lids, approx. heights without handles 10cm, diameter 21cm, Bamenda Museum, November 1983

29 Soup bowls were hooked on the kitchen wall, Foumban Museum, March 1993

30 Specimens of former oil lamps, Bamessing-Ntukwe, February 1992

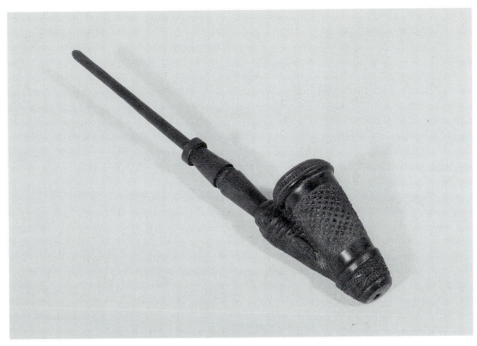

31   Commoner's tobacco pipe, Bamessing-Ntukwe, February 1984

32   Potters Fomba Africa and Keh Bamessing Keh, Bamessing-Mbeghang, March 1984

33 The pipehead is shaped with the help of a piece of wood, Bamessing-Mbeghang, June 1980.

34 The pipebowl is hollowed out to hold the tobacco, Bamessing-Mbeghang, June 1980.

35 Modelling the figure's headgear, Bamessing–Mbeghang, November 1983

36 The firing is prepared, Bamessing–Mbeghang, December 1983.

37 Short and inadequate firing, Bamessing–Mbeghang, December 1983

38   Short and inadequate firing, Bamessing-Mbeghang, December 1983

39   Choking the fire, Bamessing-Mbeghang, December 1983

40   Red pieces from the raphia rootstock, Bamessing–
Mbeghang, December 1983

41   The pieces of raphia pith are hammered, Bamessing-Mbeghang, December 1983.

42   The bundles of fibres are wrung out in water, Bamessing–Mbeghang, December 1983.

43   Blackening process, Bamessing–Mbeghang, December 1983

44 Potter Susanna Bei from Bamessing-Mbeleng carrying her products to the weekly Bamessing market, Bamessing, January 1992

45 Bamessing pots being head-loaded by trader Kwebele Mbuta from Bamessing-Ntenka, for sale as far away as Widikum, Bali-Nyonga, December 1983

THE WEAVING OF RAPHIA FIBRES

The two renowned centres for raphia weaving in the Western Grasslands are the Chiefdoms of Bamessing and Meta'. Up to the present day, the versatile raphia fibre bag is an everyday necessity for men, women and children alike, though the bags may serve different purposes and vary somewhat in size and appearance.

Men usually carry plain practical shoulder bags for personal belongings (1). The strap of the shoulder bag is lifted over the left arm, shoulder and head, and placed on the right shoulder so that the bag hangs down the left side. Thus the right hand and arm are ensured free movement. The strap consists of ten loosely twisted fibres which are bundled and fastened on either end to the two top corners of the bag.

When a man goes to the farm or the raphia grove, the shoulder bag helps him to carry his sheathed cutlass (2), his multipurpose knife, his drinking horn, some cola nuts, snuff, in former times his tobacco pipe, tobacco and lighter (the latter consisting of a small flat iron, bent into a rectangle, a flint and some tinder from the oil palm) and some money. When going to a meeting house (3) or a death celebration (4), a man takes a better looking bag, in which he carries the very same personal things, except the cutlass.

The handbag of a dignitary or member of a traditional society has the handle in the shape of a loop attached to the centre of the front and back of the bag - not the two sides and corners. These bags bear figurative designs, such as people, animals (5, 6) and double gongs (7). Bags with applied ornament, be they small woven protruding pouches or designs made with sisal hemp fibres, show the man to be a member of ngumba (8). A traditional dignitary hardly ever carries his bag himself. A boy follows a few steps behind him carrying the bag and sometimes his gun. When a woman goes to the farm she does not carry a bag but a basket. In it she stores her short-handled hoe, cooked food for her husband and herself (fufu, cocoyam, bush plums), cola nuts, her snuff, tobacco pipe with its accessories, her drinking calabash and sometimes seeds. When coming back from the farm in the evening, she most probably has to carry her basket filled with some kind of farm produce, and a head-load of firewood tied on top.

When a woman goes to the market she carries a basket filled with farm produce for sale on her head or in a back-basket (as is the case in the Moghamo/Widikum area, and from Bafut Obang via Befang to Esimbi) and at the same time a fibre handbag on her left arm. This bag contains her few personal belongings such as her drinking calabash, tobacco pipe with accessories, cola nuts and money. She carries this same bag with the same contents without a basket on her head, when she goes to a meeting house.

A boy who goes on errands for his father always carries a fibre bag. Among pupils and college students the most widespread schoolbag is the fibre bag for carrying school books, writing and drawing utensils. A child's bag may be either a shoulder bag or a handbag.

In palaces and society houses large-size fibre bags serve the purpose of storing and transporting objects used for tribal dances, medicines, charms and suchlike, when removed from their secret hiding places, because these objects must not be seen by women (9).

RAPHIA PALM

Though commonly called 'bamboo', the raphia is a tropical evergreen woody plant with large feathery fronds and belongs to the family of *Palmae*. The sole raw material used in bag-weaving is obtained from the leaflets (pinnae) of the raphia palm. There are two main species of raphia palm existing in the North West Province: the commonly called *mbu raphia* (*Raphia gaertneri*) and the *ñka raphia* (*Raphia pedunculata*). The latter is the most common one and preferred as a source of fibres for weaving. In both weaving centres, Bamessing and Meta', the *Raphia pedunculata* is the only one available.

In search of fibres, the weaver goes from plant to plant in the raphia grove looking for new leaves which have shot high up but have not opened yet (10). He grips the leaf-stem as high up as possible, shaking it hard. The 'package' opens and the pale yellow-greenish, translucent leaflets appear forming the pinnate leaf (11). These young, fresh leaflets are what the weaver wants. He collects them from many new leaves but only removes the leaflets of the middle part of the leaf, whereas he leaves the leaflets at the apex and the base of the leaf untouched on the rhachis (12). He does so for two reasons. Firstly, the leaflets on either end are of lesser quality for the weaver, and secondly, the rhachis needs the upper leaflets for further growth. On a medium-sized embryo leaf of 4.5m length, 72 leaflets were removed from the centre part. Out of the lot 42 were around 1.9m long and thirty between 1.5 and 1.6m. Seventy-six leaflets were left on the leaf, namely 64 at the apex and 12 at the base. In this way, no harm is done to the plant even if leaflets of two or three leaves per plant are taken at any one time.

The collected leaflets are bundled up and carried home (13). Next they are sorted by length (14). The longest leaflets in the bundle that Isaac Kwati from Tikali quarter (Bali-Nyonga) carried home one day in 1993 were 2.1m long (15) and 5cm wide (16). It is the fibrous epidermis which is used in raphia weaving. The weaver, Daniel Ngari took over this particular consignment of leaflets. He removed the epidermis from the rest of the leaflet (the thicker, softer mesophyll) by the following method.

- He held the bottom of the leaflet firmly under his left foot.
- In order to get a hold on the epidermis, he bent back the top 10cm of the leaflet, with the epidermis on top of the curve, the mesophyll underneath. This compressed the mesophyll and damaged it in such a way that he could obtain a separate grip on the two parts of the leaflet and pull the mesophyll away from the epidermis (17).
- Separating about 20cm of the epidermis from the mesophyll, he used both thumb nails to split it into small 'eyes' (threads) and then removed its full length (17).

When he was through with the whole bundle he hung the fibres on a horizontal pole to dry them in the sun. These sun-dried fibres are the best for tying and weaving.

DYEING OF RAPHIA FIBRES

The Meta' weavers use only chemical dyes available in powder form on the local market. The Bamessing weavers use both natural and chemical dyes. The speciality of most Bamessing weavers is the well-known bags woven in black and white. The black colour is a natural dye obtained in the following way. The fibres are boiled up with leaves of the red bush plum tree, in pidgin English *bush butter* (*Pachylobus edulis* or *Dacryodes edulis*) for half an hour. No change is yet visible. The pot with the hot brew is carried to the nearest raphia grove and buried there in black mud (18) letting it stay over night. Having removed the fibres, the still muddy product must be thoroughly washed, preferably in the current of a stream, until the deep black colour shows up (19).

In the absence of plum leaves, some Bamessing weavers use the leaves of a shrub called *fessia* (20) (*Ficus* spp) which are plentiful on the hillsides. In Bafut, besides the plum leaves (*ajoh*), the leaves of a tree called *nubue* are also used. The procedure and result are the same as with the plum leaves.

The green colour is obtained from the fresh leaves of the mango tree and the pumpkin plant. They are pounded in a mortar and boiled with the fibres. The result is a light green colour.

Pink, green, and brown colours can also be obtained. The relevant plant is called *mọsisi* in Mụngaka, *kaa* in Bafut and *fekang* in Nsei (*Acanthaceae*, possibly *Hypoestes*). The green plants are boiled up with the raphia fibres which will turn them pink. Adding wood ashes to the brew changes the pink to green. If the boiling is continued for another 30 minutes the fibres assume a brownish colour. In former times, ink was made out of the *mọsisi* plant by wrapping its leaves in green fresh banana leaves and putting it into fire for a few minutes. The result is a thick, violet liquid which must still be diluted with water to form ink.

Yellow is got from the bark of a tree called *gogha* in the Mụngaka, *njamunwi* in the Bafut, *kefodi* in the Nsei, and *eserembenbu* in the Meta' languages. The outer, rough part of the bark is cleaned off and the inner soft part pounded in a mortar then boiled with the raphia fibres for about thirty minutes. The result is yellow fibres. In

Meta' the innermost part of the bark is chewed raw as medicine against coughs. In Nsei the pulp got from ground leaves of the *kefodi* tree is used for the treatment of wounds. A strong bright yellow is also got from the small tubers of the plant called *nya* in the Nsei language.

Red colour is obtained from camwood (*Baphia sp.*) and padouk wood (*Pterocarpus sp.*), the seeds of the avocado fruit (*Persea gratissima*) cola nuts (*Cola anomala*) and the bark and roots of the tree called *muntsintsi*, and *nkatoli* in the Mungaka and Bafut languages respectively.

A pleasant orange/red colour is obtained from the pulpy seeds in the ripe, but still fresh, capsules of the Annatto tree (*Bixa orellana*) (21). The seeds are pounded and the resulting pulp added to the fibres and boiled for 30-40 minutes.

The deep blue indigo dye, obtained from plants found in the north of Cameroon, seems to be the sole source of the colour blue. All our experiments concerning blue, and using local plants, have been to no avail. Interestingly enough, the fibres assume a pink colour when boiled with the blue-violet *mosisi* brew from which violet ink can be made.

THE WEAVING OF RAPHIA FIBRES

A two-bar loom is used for the weaving of raphia fibres. The warp length is determined by the length of the fibres which are equal to the length of the leaflets. (I mentioned earlier leaflets of 2.1m length, but in general, the majority of the leaflets are somewhat below 2m.)

In Bamessing and Meta', the weaving of raphia fibres is done by men. In Meta' weaving is mainly done in Bome and Njah-Etu, and in Bamessing in the two quarters of Ntukwe and Mbesoh. All stages including the searching for leaflets, preparation of the fibres, weaving and sewing of the finished article are carried out by men (22), most of whom belong to families which have been engaged in this occupation for generations.

Some weavers are owners of their own raphia palm groves whereas others have to buy either the fresh leaflets or the dry fibres on the local market. In the early 1980s, the Bamessing weavers were almost ruined when the largest stand of raphia palms in the Chiefdom was recklessly bulldozed and changed into a rice-farm by a French development organisation. Barely half a dozen years later the rice market collapsed throughout the country so that staff were cut from about 260 to 60. In addition, the seven expatriates were withdrawn from the project so that many Bamessing men were deprived of their income, both from the weaving of raphia fibres and the growing of rice. Ever since, those Bamessing weavers who did not give up their craft have had to buy their fibres from Bamali or Bambalang farmers. The unavoidable consequence was a rise in the price of woven articles.

The Loom, Warp and Weft

The process and technology of raphia weaving are fully described in V. and A. Lamb (1981) to which the reader is referred. A brief outline here will suffice.

For raphia-weaving, an upright, single-heddle loom is used, made of raphia wood. Average dimensions are 1.5m high by 60cm broad. Top and bottom of the warp are attached to crossbars and the whole structure is portable and is used leant against a convenient prop such as a tree or wall.

The weaver begins by sorting the raphia fibres into bundles. In Bamessing this is commonly 13-16 bundles of 18 threads, the exact number depending on the width of the weft (23). Each is folded so that it now contains 36 threads.

Weaving

Weaving requires only a shed stick, a heddle and a weaving sword. Heddle and shed stick are opposed, with the sword stick used for opening and beating. Unusually, the weft thread is not attached to the shuttle but passed through the shed by hand. Since raphia threads are very short, a continuous weft is excluded. An individual thread may be used at each pass, with the ends left free or a selvage may be created by making several passes with a single thread.

A textile of this form lends itself easily to decoration with coloured stripes both in the warp and weft. This is something of a speciality of

Meta' weavers. Stripes of bright yellow, orange, green, blue and purple are common.

Bamessing weavers, on the other hand, have recently tended to greater use of supplementary floating weft decoration, so that they produce representational images of people, animals (24), houses and scenery on both raphia bags and 'tapestries'. The technique involves the production of a sort of negative image by colouring in the background with supplementary wefts, using a thin pointed stick, so that the image appears in uncoloured raphia. Another recent innovation is the production of raphia bags bearing the name or map of Cameroon.

In Bamessing the members of *nwa ghugh* (upper *ngumba*) have a special bag which nobody else must use. This fibre bag is usually red and the front is covered with rectangular pouches. The effect is as if the bag has been covered with small amulet containers. The raphia pouches are produced by extending the warp at regular intervals to make flaps which are later sewn up into the pouch form. These pouches open on the inside of the bag and they can be used to hold charms and magical substances (8 left). Tufted bags (8 right) are also produced in Bamessing. The tufts are applied during weaving, each row is separated from the next by intermediate weft tabby throws. Today sisal hemp fibres are more often used than raphia fibres to make tufts; and these are dyed with chemical dyes to yield all sorts of colours, red, orange, black and blue in various shades. Sisal tufts, particularly when trimmed short, give a much softer, almost velvet-like feel than do raphia fibres (25).

For the most part fibre bags are made square, ranging from 34 x 34 to 40 x 40cm (there are, however, bigger and smaller ones available). For a bag measuring 40 x 40 a web of 80cm length and 40cm width is required. After weaving the web is cut off the loom by means of a razor blade, folded into two equal parts and sewn up along the selvedges. All the edges are hemmed with fibres, the top corners provided with tufts and the bottom two corners with tassels in the case of Bamessing bags. Two single loop-shaped black handles are fitted vertically in the centres of the two faces. On prestige bags, the braided handle ropes open up into large tassels which are longer and more voluminous than the corner tassels. In most cases, the handles, tufts and tassels are made not from raphia fibres but from the fibres extracted from the stem of a special type of banana, the *Bakwele* banana, as the Bamessing weavers call it. I was told that it is a special type of banana imported from down south, the Bakweri land, probably from a plantation.

Most of the weaving is done indoors. That is why weavers are seldom seen by visitors. Since the extreme dryness of the air in the peak months of the dry season (December, January and February) makes the warp fibres break, weaving is done then in the cool of the early mornings and late evenings only. Some full-time weavers move to a cool place with their looms and fibres during that hot, dry period, namely into a thick bush where one will find them weaving on the bank of a stream.

The Meta' bags are different from the Bamessing bags in both appearance and technique. The Bamessing bag is made of one width only while the Meta' bag consists of two. Face, back and inner partition are two different widths. The coloured face is woven more finely than the plain and coarser back. Although face and back are two different pieces, each one is woven twice the length of a bag. After weaving, the long, coloured, outward-facing width is cut into two halves and used for two bags, whereas the long coarser back width is folded and joined to the facing width. On joining the parts together they are sewn up not only along the selvedges, as is the case in Bamessing, but also along the bottom edge. In this way the Meta' bag is provided with a useful inner partition. Two coils wrapped in coloured fibres are tied in with the selvedges. The projecting upper ends of the coils are curved inside and, with the ten loose shoulder strap twines, joined together into a long cylindrical tuft which is meticulously wound round with tiny coloured fibre twines (26).

In both Chiefdoms, Bamessing and Meta', the output of raphia fibre bags of one kind or another is considerable. Producers take their bags to the weekly market - Tad market (27) and Bamessing market respectively - where they are bought in bulk by traders and distributed all over the country. The raphia bag with or without inscription, in the case of Bamessing, is probably the most common gift given to visitors by a *Fon*, Chief, group, congregation or individual. During a marriage, the couple must certainly be given distinctive raphia bags, the bride a good-looking handbag and the bridegroom a handsome shoulder-bag.

The Meta' weavers produce three main types of raphia fibre bags. Marcus Tata (born *c.* 1935) from Kup-Bome is renowned for being the master weaver of the coloured bags, called *parama*, Josef Munuh (born *c.* 1930) from Fenam-Bome is known as the best weaver of the white bag with the pleasant green/red stripe pattern, called *abamakon*, and Peter Mamisang (born *c.* 1919) from Baraji-Bome produces the best big and strong bags, called *abamengi*, which are of a coarser weave than the other two more elegant types (28). Each of the three master weavers has his own school. They are the ones who began supplying me with the said three types of Meta' bags when my interest first began in the early 1960s.

For dyeing fibres, they say that they prefer chemical to natural colours for three reasons: first, the chemical colours are easily available from traders who bring them from Nigeria; second, they are less labour intensive; and third, they are brighter. In former times, when they were using natural dyes, their bags were made in three colours only: green, black and yellow because these three dyes were relatively easily available, whereas red was difficult and expensive to get from camwood. (Annatto was not known in this region until I imported it from Nigeria in 1961.)

Prescraft had an even more reviving effect on the Bamessing raphia fibre weaving industry from 1961. Bonuses were introduced for weavers who produced prime quality bags and above all, were able to trace out old traditional designs. The result was a considerable increase in the diversity of designs. In the mid 1960s when Cameroon became alive with tourists, picturesque wall-hangings were in demand in addition to the figurative bags and since these offer more space than the bags, they can be used to show short stories. The last weaving competition at Bamessing in which over 30 weavers participated, most of them from Ntukwe quarter, was organised in September 1989 with remarkable results (29).

In his book, *Art of Cameroon*, Paul Gebauer shows 19 raphia fibre bags and 4 tapestries, all of the clear typical Bamessing style. Surprisingly, none of the 23 pieces is said to originate from Bamessing. He attributes 19 pieces to Bamunka, 1 to Bikom, 1 to Foumbot, 1 to Foumban and 1 to Bangolan. It seems strange that such a connoisseur of the Western Grassland's arts and crafts makes no reference to Bamessing whatsoever.

While stationed at Bamessing, I contacted a good number of knowledgeable Bamessing men in this matter. I was repeatedly referred to a native of Bamessing working at Bamunka, Nunia Mbinyi Daniel (born *c.* 1930, or earlier). He was not a stranger to me for I had made his acquaintance sometime in the 1960s when I wanted to have a young Bali-Nyonga man trained by him in raphia weaving. Daniel Mbinyi retired in 1988 after he had served the Government School Ndop as a handicraft teacher for almost 40 years. He told me his life-story as follows. He was born around 1930 in Ntukwe-Nsei (Bamessing). As a boy between seven and ten years of age he entered the then N.A. (Native Authority) School in Ndop in 1937. (The School was opened in 1927 and in 1971 it became a Government school.) In 1948 he passed the First School Leaving Certificate Examination while in Standard Six. When Daniel Mbinyi, somewhere between seven and ten years old, left his father's compound at Ntukwe to start schooling at Bamunka in 1937, he took with him his loom on which he had learnt to weave the well known Bamessing bags. While in school he developed a special skill in handicrafts in general and in raphia fibre weaving in particular. One day in the year 1948 the Trusteeship Committee of the United Nations visited Nigeria of which Southern Cameroon was then part. Since the team also reached Bamenda, the Senior Divisional Officer in Bamenda, Mr Kay, in conjunction with the then Education Officer, Mr Too Good (*sic*), were looking for a souvenir for the visiting team. They approached the Headmaster of the N.A. School Ndop who asked Daniel Mbinyi to weave the map of the Bamenda Division (the now North West Province). Daniel Mbinyi was then in Standard Six and had already studied the maps of Africa, Cameroon and Bamenda. He carried out the assignment successfully and the souvenir was handed over to the visiting team by the Acting Governor in Buea. The latter was so impressed by this piece of art that he asked the Senior Divisional Officer in Bamenda to see to it that the producer was sent for further training in arts and crafts. This was done, Daniel Mbinyi was sent to the craft centre at Ekot-Ekpene in Nigeria, where he underwent a six-month course in general weaving and other crafts from January to June 1949. On his return from training, Daniel Mbinyi was employed in his former school as a full-time handicraft teacher. Two years later he was sent back to Ekot-Ekpene for another training course and after completion he resumed his duty as handicraft teacher in his former school, a post he held until his retirement in 1988.

As to Gebauer's *Art of Cameroon*, with special reference to the section on raphia fibre weaving, Daniel Mbinyi had the following to say:

Though Bamessing is nowhere mentioned, all fibre articles shown in the book with the exception of two are pieces of the classical Bamessing style. This type of weaving technique as well as the designs are peculiar to Bamessing and are nowhere else known and practised. I was the one who introduced the Bamessing weaving in the N.A. School Ndop as from 1937. I can say with all certainty that these pieces were woven by me or my pupils. As to the bags which P. Gebauer collected in other places than Bamunka, e.g. in Bikom, Foumbot, Foumban and Bangolan, they were undoubtedly produced in Ntukwe-Bamessing and taken to the markets of these places by traders for sale.

To the question why P. Gebauer did not make mention of Bamessing, I must say that to my knowledge he had never been to Bamessing because there was no establishment of his denomination there. But he often came to the handicraft section of the school where I was teaching. Many a time he asked me to follow him to Bamenda to work for him there; but I refused. So he just continued to come from time to time to buy our crafts. He was the one who started asking for 'wall pictures', 'tapestries' as they are now called. Originally the Bamessing weavers made all their raphia fibre webs into bags.

During almost 40 years of experience as pupil and teacher I rarely found non-Bamessing boys interested in the art of Bamessing weaving. If one or the other endeavoured to learn it, it was because they wanted to learn how to weave what they liked most: to produce a bag with their name on it.

The oldest living weaver in Ntukwe, Ba Yangeh, who is a member of a number of traditional societies in Bamessing furnished me with the following information on the four pieces which Gebauer said to have been bought in Bikom, Foumbot, Foumban and Bangolan respectively.

One of them is a normal size (38 x 38cm) prestige bag which can only be used by a dignitary on public occasions, such as market, meetings, death celebrations. No others than members of one of the following traditional societies are entitled to own and use a bag such as this (30):
- *Fung* (kingmakers, sub-chiefs, members of *Nwua*; which is *Ngumba*);
- *Nwua-Kwe* (which is Upper *Ngumba* or *KwiFon*);
- *Nwua-Betu* (Night *Ngumba*) and *Nwua-Bia* (Red *Ngumba*).

Members of these societies use such bags only when not on duty for their society. The proper bags for use within the society contain all sorts of medicines and charms. These bags are made differently, for instance provided with a good number of small pouches or applied sisal hemp designs on the faces of the bags (8, 31). Bags of these kinds can only be woven by a society member. Ba Kehindo used to weave them right up till his death around 1955 as did Ba Yangeh, who is still alive, but too weak to weave a good bag.

In the Cameroon arts collection of the Dahlem Museum in Berlin, I discovered large raphia bags of the Bamessing type woven in black and white (e.g. 56cm long x 75cm wide). I photographed nine bags, three of which are shown here, and an unfinished one in 1975 (32). These large bags consist of four woven pieces sewn together. The ten photographed pieces depict ten different geometrical patterns.

The bags are said to originate from Bamoum and to have been collected there in 1908. It may seem odd that Bamessing bags were obtained in Foumban but Bamessing oral tradition says that the farm of the Sultan of Foumban extended to the Ndop Plain, of which Bamessing is part, until after the end of World War I.

RAPHIA TEXTILES

In the almost four decades of my stay in Cameroon, I have come across only one man who produces raphia textiles. He is Abasi Dele (born *c.* 1920), native of Bamessing-Mbesoh quarter, and a farmer, carpenter and weaver. He learnt raphia fibre weaving from his father. To my knowledge he is one of the very few weavers in Bamessing who exclusively use natural dye-stuffs to colour the raphia fibres. The red colour he gets from camwood, the yellow colour from the tubers of the plant called *nya* and the black colour from the leaves of the tree called *fessia* mixed with black mud. His well-tailored trousers and waist-coat were designed and made by him for the National Agricultural Show at Bamenda in 1984 (33, 34).

When I asked Abesi Dele whether there was a market for such raphia textiles, he said, 'I have produced and sold just a few suits, but in actual fact there is no market yet for raphia textiles.'

In addition to occasional textiles, Abasi Dele weaves handbags and shoulder-bags.

22 Weaving and sewing Bamessing bags, Bamessing–Ntukwe, September 1989

1 and 2   Men with plain practical shoulder bags, Bali-Nyonga, 1976

3 and 4   Colourfully designed bags are worn during traditional festivals, Bali-Nyonga, 1992 and 1993.

5 Black and white Bamessing bag with figurative designs,
Bamessing-Ntukwe, September 1989

6 Black and white Bamessing bag with figurative designs, in the compound of Chief
J.C. Kangsen, then also Moderator of the Presbyterian Church in Cameroon, Wum,
January 1982.

7 Black and white Bamessing bag with the double gong
design, Bamessing-Ntukwe, September 1989

8 Left: bag with woven protruding pouches. Right: bag with an extra layer of
tufts made of sisal hemp fibres, Bali-Nyonga, May 1992

9 Large-sized fibre bag for storing and transporting ritual objects, on the occasion of a grand death celebration at Mboh, Bali-Nyonga, March 1993

10 In search of fresh raphia leaflets, Bali-Nyonga, November 1972

11 A young pinnate raphia leaf, Bali-Nyonga, February 1993

12 Leaflets have been taken from the middle part of the leaf, upper and lower leaflets remain, Bali-Nyonga, February 1993.

13　　Weaver Abraham Yoh carrying a bundle of leaflets home, Bamessing-Ntukwe, September 1989

14　Weaver Daniel Ngari Tefe sorting the leaflets according to their length, Bali-Nyonga, February 1993

15　Isaac Kwati with leaflets 210cm long in his right hand, Bali-Nyonga, February 1993

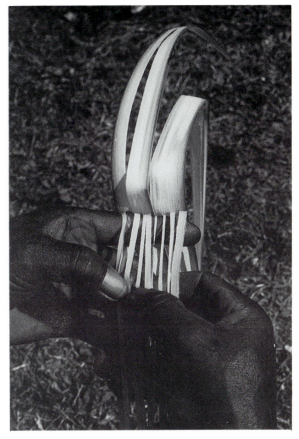

16 The leaflets when unfolded are 4–5cm broad, Bali-Nyonga, February 1993.

17 Removing and splitting the epidermis, preparatory to weaving, Bali-Nyonga, March 1993

18 Weaver Martin Ngubui burying the cooked fibres in black mud, Bamessing-Ntukwe, September 1989

19   Weaver Martin Ngubui washing the blackened fibres, Bamessing-Ntukwe, September 1989

20   A shrub called fessia, Bamessing-Ntukwe, September 1989.

21   The Annatto tree, Prescraft Bali-Nyonga, February 1993

Note: *For illustration 22 see page 91.*

23   Fixing raphia bundles onto the loom,
Bamessing-Ntukwe, September 1989

25 Raphia bag with sisal tufts on it, Bamessing-Mbeghang, 1984

24 Black and white Bamessing raphia panel, Bali-Nyonga, September 1992

26 Colourful tuft on a Meta' bag, Tad market, May 1992

27 Meta' bags at the Tad market, May 1992

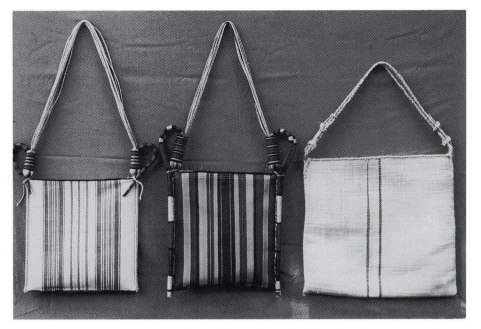

28   The three different types of Meta' bags: from the left, *abamakon, parama, abamengi*, Tad market, May 1992

29   Some of the participants in the weaving competition, Bamessing-Ntukwe, September 1989

30   Black and white Bamessing bag belonging to a
dignitary, Bamessing-Ntukwe, September 1989

31   Raphia bag with an applied design made of sisal
fibres, Oku-Ngashie, January 1992

32a and b   Raphia bags in the Dahlem Museum, Berlin, October 1975

32c above, and d right: Raphia bags in the Dahlem Museum, Berlin, October 1975

33   Tailored raphia waistcoat made by Abesi Dele, Bamessing-Ntukwe, February 1992

34   Abesi Dele clad in tailored raphia textiles, Bamessing-Ntukwe, February 1992

GLOSSARY AND ABBREVIATIONS

Chop-chair	Pidgin-English expression for a successor, i.e. someone who will 'chop' (chop = eat) an office symbolised by a chair or throne
Cocoyam	A food plant having edible underground tubers
Cowry	The glossy, brightly marked shell with an elongated opening of any marine gastropod mollusc, especially the shell of *cypraea moneta* (money cowry) which were used as money in parts of Africa dn South Asia, (from Hindi *Kauri*).
CWF	Christian Women's Fellowship of the Presbyterian Church in Cameroon
Dane gun	A muzzle-loading gun with flintlock
Fon	The traditional ruler of a large ethnic group or *Fondom*
Fufu	Mainly corn *fufu* made from maize flour boiled in water and eaten with hot soup, often the staple food
Fulani	A nomadic pastoral people of West and Central Africa, living chiefly in the sub-Sahara region from Senegal to North Cameroon
Juju	1. An object superstitiously revered and used as a charm or fetish; 2. the powers associated with a *juju*; 3. a taboo effected by a *juju*; 4. any process in which a mystery is exploited to confuse people; 5. 'the mask' i.e. dancer, wooden head and costume as an entity.
Kenja	A pidgin-English word for a longish basket made in hexagonal plait and used as a portable hen house or for packing pots for transport
Kingmakers	In most ethnic groups there are seven kingmakers, in some others there are nine. They have a number of important functions:

Kingmakers (continued):

1 They can touch and carry the *Fon* when he is ill but only after special cleansing rites.
2 When the *Fon* is outside the palace, they can accompany him and provide him with food. No one else may see the *Fon* eat.
3 They carry secret messages, for example his last will and testament.
4 If the *Fon* 'has gone on a long journey' before naming his successor, they appoint the new *Fon*.
5 They protect the *Fon* against enemies and rivals within and outside the royal family.
6 During an interregnum they take care of the *Fon's* property until his replacement is enthroned.
7 They settle disputes between rivals. If the case is beyond them, they pass it to the *KwiFon* society.

KwiFon	The executive body of traditional government, consisting of senior members of the community. Its functions are:

KwiFon (continued):

1 To carry our rituals.
2 To protect the palace and its laws.
3 To ensure the fertility of humans, fields and livestock.
4 To pass and execute judgement in serious cases.

The *Fon* is subject to *KwiFon* which acts as a counterbalance to his own power. The word *KwiFon* is from *kwi* 'ripe', 'mature' and *Fon* 'ruler'. The Fon is called *mu KwiFon* 'son of *KwiFon*', meaning that the power of the Fon comes from *KwiFon*.

Manilla	An early form of currency in West Africa in the form of a small bracelet.
Manjong	A pidgin-English word for societies or associations other than the so-called great or regulatory societies e.g. in Bali-Nyonga the following societies fall under this term: *Mandet, Langa, Makoni, Njiba*, whereas *Ngumba, Voma and Ngwe* are secret societies with nocturnal activities.
Mimbo	A pidgin-English word for the palm wine tapped from oil palms, raphia palms and wild date palms - usually called white *mimbo*. It is also used to refer to beverages in general.
Mungaka	The present language of the Bali-Nyonga people
Ngumba	Pidgin-English for *KwiFon*
Nsei	The pre-colonial name for Bamessing
Plantain	A large tropical plant (*Musa paradisiaca*) with green-skinned, banana-like fruit, eaten as a staple food
Prescraft	Abbreviation for the Presbyterian Handicraft Centre started in Bafut in 1961
Prespot	Abbreviation for the Presbyterian Pottery Project started in Bamessing in 1983
Rhachis	The main axis of a pinnate compound leaf
Tad market	The main weekly market in Meta' held every eighth day according to the traditional eight-day week

BIBLIOGRAPHY

Allen, H.C., unpubl. 'A study of the feasibility of introducing high-temperature glazed pottery production to the region of Bamenda/Bali'.

Breton, R. and Fohtung, B., 1991, *Atlas administratif des langues nationales du Cameroun*. Yaounde: CREA.

Fröhlich, M., 1979, *Gelbgiesser im Kameruner Grasland: Ein technologischer Bericht*. Zurich: Museum Rietberg.

Gebauer, P., 1979, *Art of Cameroon*. Portland, Oregon: Portland Art Museum.

Herbert, E., 1990, 'Lost-wax casting in the Cameroon Grasslands', in *West African Economic and Social History; Studies in Memory of Marion Johnson*, eds D. Henige and T. McCaskie. Madison: University of Wisconsin Press.

Lamb, V. and A., 1981, *Au Cameroun: Weaving - Tissage*. Cameroon: Elf Serepca.

Marfurt, L., n.d. 'Pipes du Cameroun', numero hors-serie de *Recherches et Etudes Camerounaises*.

Nkwi, P., 1976, *Traditional Government and Social Change*. Fribourg: Fribourg University Press.

Nkwi, P. and Warnier J.-P., 1982, *A History of the Western Grassfields*. Publication of the Department of Sociology, University of Yaounde.

Valentin, P. 1981, 'Töpferwaren aus Bamessing (Kamerun),' *Sonderdruck aus Tribus*, no. 30.